PMS

A POSITIVE PROGRAM TO GAIN CONTROL

PMS

A POSITIVE PROGRAM TO GAIN CONTROL

Stephanie DeGraff Bender
Kathleen Kelleher

Foreword by Terri F. Rosenbaum, M.D.
Fellow, American College of Obstetrics & Gynecology

Illustrations by Caron Elizabeth Dunn

THE BODY PRESS

Published by **The Body Press**
A Division of HPBooks, Inc.
P.O. Box 5367, Tucson, AZ 85703 (602) 888-2150
ISBN 0-89586-465-7 Library of Congress Catalog Number 86-62073
 Printed in U.S.A.
1st Printing

Technical Consultants:

Rene Allen, M.D.
Fellow, American College of Obstetrics & Gynecology
Martie Fankhauser, M.S.
Clinical Assistant Professor
Department of Pharmacy Practice, College of Pharmacy
Department of Psychiatry, College of Medicine
University of Arizona
Tucson, Arizona

Dedication

For my husband, Bill Bender, and my sons, Billy and Tim—the most loving support system I'll ever have.

Stephanie DeGraff Bender

For my mother, Mary Jo Kelleher, and my seven sisters—each a strong and loving woman.

Kathleen Kelleher

Contents

Acknowledgements

We would like to express our heartfelt thanks for help and moral support during the course of this project to Judith Wesley Allen, Caron Dunn, Bill Bender, Terri Rosenbaum, Rowena Stout, Gloria O'Reilly, Jim Blanford, Eric Smith, and all the women who have sought help at the PMS Clinic.

Foreword

Many times a doctor doesn't have time to counsel patients about the psychological and emotional dynamics of premenstrual syndrome. Yet most of my patients with PMS tell me that their psychological symptoms are the most troublesome part of the problem. For this reason, I often refer my patients for counseling.

Stephanie Bender, director of the PMS Clinic in Boulder, Colorado, has counseled hundreds of women about the changes that develop in their relationships due to PMS. At the PMS Clinic a woman can learn to overcome the very problems that make it difficult for her to help herself. Stephanie helps her focus on the emotional issues and shows her how to turn potentially troublesome social situations into beneficial ones. She also educates a woman about the importance of diet, vitamins, exercise and support systems. She has helped many patients regain a positive sense of self-esteem and begin to enjoy life again.

Because many women don't know about PMS, and there is much misunderstanding about PMS in the medical profession, a woman can fear that her bewildering PMS-related behavior means that she is "going crazy" or that she has a "depressed personality." A woman can feel so embarrassed about her behavior that she is reluctant to talk to anyone—even her doctor—about it.

Sadly, the result of her silence can be alienation of friends and family, as well as feelings of personal guilt, inadequacy and hopelessness. Many of my PMS patients have reached this stage before coming to me for help. In some cases, a woman has already lost husband and friends—the very people to whom she could have turned for understanding and support had she recognized PMS earlier.

The major contribution of this book is that it addresses the important issues for women who suffer from PMS: emotional distress, relationship and family dynamics, and professional concerns. The authors talk to women in a believable and sensitive way.

If you are suffering from PMS and it is still in the early stages, reading this book will help you recognize the pattern of your emotional ups and downs. The dynamics that you are most likely experiencing in your relationships at home and work will come into clearer focus. You can take comfort from the fact that you are hardly alone—you are suffering from one of the most common maladies that has traditionally affected womankind. You can then start to act in your own behalf and begin to regain control through self-help measures.

If you were my patient and you were suffering from PMS, I would point out to you that if you broke a leg and had to wear a cast for several months, you would need to relearn to use your leg once the cast was removed. In a similar vein, once the physical symptoms of PMS are treated, you need to treat the psychological aftermath. Your relationships may need rehabilitation, and you may need to learn to interact with people again in a positive way. Now that this book is available, I suggest that you use it as a tool to getting better and repairing damage in your life.

The medical profession is learning to identify PMS and offer some help, but there are differences of opinion as to what causes PMS. We do know that PMS can exacerbate already-existing physical and psychological disorders. If the suggestions in this book about diet, vitamins, exercise, and other self-help measures do not lessen your physical discomfort or emotional distress, it is probably time for medical consultation. Chart your symptoms so you can share this information with your doctor. Daily charts are extremely valuable to your doctor in diagnosing a problem—whether or not there is a clear pattern to the symptoms.

PMS is only one of many disorders that can affect your physical health. Several other disorders—especially ones that affect your endocrine system—have symptoms similar to those of PMS. These include hypothyroidism, benign adrenal tumors and pituitary dysfunction. Although there are no blood tests that determine if you have PMS, blood tests can help your doctor determine if some of these other problems are present.

Likewise, a number of conditions can affect your emotional/psychological state. PMS is just one of them. Others include psychosis, manic-depression and severe depression. These also can cause symptoms similar to PMS. Although there are no psychological tests that determine if you have PMS, psychological tests can help determine if some of these other problems are present. However, these tests are expensive. Because of this, I try to discover first if a woman's symptoms are occurring in a regular pattern with respect to her menstrual cycle. If her charts suggest that she is suffering from PMS, I treat the PMS. If another problem is still present, I treat it or refer her to the appropriate specialist.

Women are insisting on better medical care. More important, we are seizing the opportunity to find out about our bodies and take better care of ourselves. Until recently, when—or if—PMS was recognized, it was often thought of in terms of "female trouble" that had to be endured. Now, if you follow the guidelines offered in this book, you can learn to help yourself before the problem becomes too severe. Thanks to books such as this, we can actively take control of our own physical and emotional well-being.

Terri F. Rosenbaum, M.D.
F.A.C.O.G.

PMS

A POSITIVE PROGRAM TO GAIN CONTROL

INTRODUCTION

In this book, we are going to focus on the emotional and psychological aspects of premenstrual syndrome (PMS). We will discuss the ways in which this medical disorder is most commonly felt by women—in their minds, hearts and interpersonal relationships. First we will talk about you: your sense of self, your emotions, your mental state and your body. Second, but just as important, we are going to talk about your relationships—your relationships with your husband or lover, your children, and the people with whom you work. We are also going to take a look at the behavior that develops when a woman has PMS over a period of time.

If you have PMS, probably what upsets you the most is that you feel you are losing control. The number-one issue—the major concern of 98 percent of the women who come to the PMS Clinic—is *loss of control*. When I ask, "What is your biggest problem with PMS?" many women respond as Laura did:

> *I'm out of control. I don't even recognize myself. It's not me. It's frightening.*

This is a scary place to be. I know because I've been there. The best way I can describe it is "predictable unpredictability." With the help of family and friends, I got through it. Many women have. So can you.

The principal goal of this book is to provide a positive approach to regaining control of PMS. If you are irritable, angry, withdrawn, overeating or drinking too much, your self-respect can plummet. No woman can experience failure on a regular basis in significant areas of her life without suffering damage to her self-esteem. This book provides insights into the effects of PMS on your life, and contains suggestions for minimizing the effects. Treatment options for PMS are explained in the final chapter. Most of these are self-help measures relating to diet, vitamins and exercise. By using this book, you can begin immediately to get a handle on the problem. You can take steps to help yourself get better.

We are going to take a team approach to PMS. The team consists of three people:

- You
- Your doctor
- Your therapist (or me, via this book)

You are the head of the team. This is because you know better than anybody—better than your doctor, better than your therapist—how you feel. You are also the one responsible for yourself, responsible for your own well-being.

In the first chapter we are going to review typical concerns that women express to me when they come to the PMS Clinic, including questions that they most frequently ask. This way, many of your questions will be answered immediately.

Then we will look at the profile of a high-risk PMS woman. You will be able to compare yourself to the typical woman who has sought counseling at the PMS Clinic.

I will ask you to fill out your personal history, just as I would if you were to visit the clinic. Then we are going to start a charting system. You can use this book to chart physical and psychological changes that you experience from month to month. I will explain how to evaluate information that you gather on your charts, and make suggestions about diet, vitamins and exercise.

After charting, if you think you have significant problems with PMS, I advise you to take a positive approach (as suggested throughout this book), as well as consult your doctor. If you talk to your doctor and your doctor says you do not have a problem, call me. I will refer you to someone in your area who can help you.

Some Hints Before Getting Started

Use this book as a step-by-step guide. The charts and exercises can help you determine if you have PMS. They are also a means for you to begin to reconstruct your life. It is very important to fill out the information as fully and accurately as possible.

Keep in mind that this is your personal book. The information you enter in this book should be as confidential as the information on the charts in my clinic. You should have a sense of privacy about this book and treat it like your diary. In this way, you can be completely open about your innermost thoughts and feelings. And you can be completely—even painfully—honest about your interactions with your family and friends.

If you think it would be helpful for your husband or other significant persons to read this book, ask them to do so before you begin recording your thoughts and feelings.

As you work with this book, remember to:

- Block out some time just for yourself.
- Take the phone off the hook.
- If you have children, arrange for someone else to take care of them.
- Tune into your relationships and think about what has happened to you in the recent past.
- Observe your body and how it has been changing.
- Trust yourself. Trust what you are thinking. Trust what you are feeling.

CHAPTER 1

What Is PMS?

Answers to Common Questions

SHEILA'S STORY

For several months in a row, I had to cancel my board meetings. I'd get a headache, it would take over, and I'd have to go to bed. I would call my husband, and he would come home and watch the kids for a day or two, because I just couldn't.

I went to a general practitioner for help, and he referred me to a neurologist. I was put on several medications. Sometimes these medications helped my headache, but they always knocked me out! So my husband still had to come home to help with the children. I also went to a pain-control center, and the doctor at the pain-control center prescribed a different drug.

After a while, I would actually plan and make special preparations for the time when I would have this debilitating headache. I would put down a plastic tablecloth in the living room and set out snacks for the kids—things that were easy to fix and eat. Then I would bring out my pillow and lie on the couch. I taped the emergency phone number to the wall. I wrote it in big numbers so the kids could read it and call their father if necessary.

One day I was on the phone explaining that I couldn't attend the board meeting and that perhaps I should resign from the board, and one of my friends overheard me. When I hung up, we started chatting. I mentioned that it was too bad that the board meetings were not in the middle of the month, because I always felt fine at that time.

My friend said, "Isn't it interesting that your headaches are always at a certain time of the month . . . the same time as the board meetings? Is this around the time of your period?"

It **was** *two days before my period. So we discussed the possibility that it was cyclical. We started piecing things together. My friend had a lot more information about PMS than I did.*

After the discussion, I decided that I had to explore every avenue. I started charting myself, and verified that my headaches were occurring only before my period. A consultation with my doctor confirmed that I was suffering from PMS.

So, it took a board meeting to find out about PMS! The board meeting was like a monthly barometer.

PMS: A MEDICAL DISORDER

What is PMS? "The world's commonest, and probably the oldest, disease"[1] is the way that one of the world's leading pioneers in the study of PMS, Dr. Katharina Dalton of the University College Hospital in London, describes this medical disorder. PMS affects a large segment of the female population of the world. It is a physical disorder that is attributed to hormonal fluctuations that take place in a woman's body. PMS often manifests itself as disturbed mood, sleep and appetite.

The fact that PMS is a physical disorder is what makes it so difficult to understand. Why? Because the psychological symptoms are the most problematic and hard to treat. It is difficult to believe that what a woman is going through is physical in origin. PMS can cause such mental stress that it shakes the foundation of her identity—who she perceives herself to be.

The *American Journal of Psychiatry* describes premenstrual syndrome as a menstrually related physical/psychological disorder that can be defined as "the cyclic occurrence of symptoms that are of sufficient severity to interfere with some aspects of life, and which appear with a consistent and predictable relationship to menses."[2]

The two aspects that are crucial to the correct definition of PMS are:

- It occurs regularly in the same phase of the menstrual cycle (between ovulation and onset of menstruation), followed by a symptom-free phase each cycle.
- The symptoms are of sufficient severity to interfere with some aspect of living.

How does PMS affect a woman?

PMS affects a woman as a cyclical emotional, behavioral and physical disturbance. Dr. Dalton has described how the numerous symptoms associated with PMS can

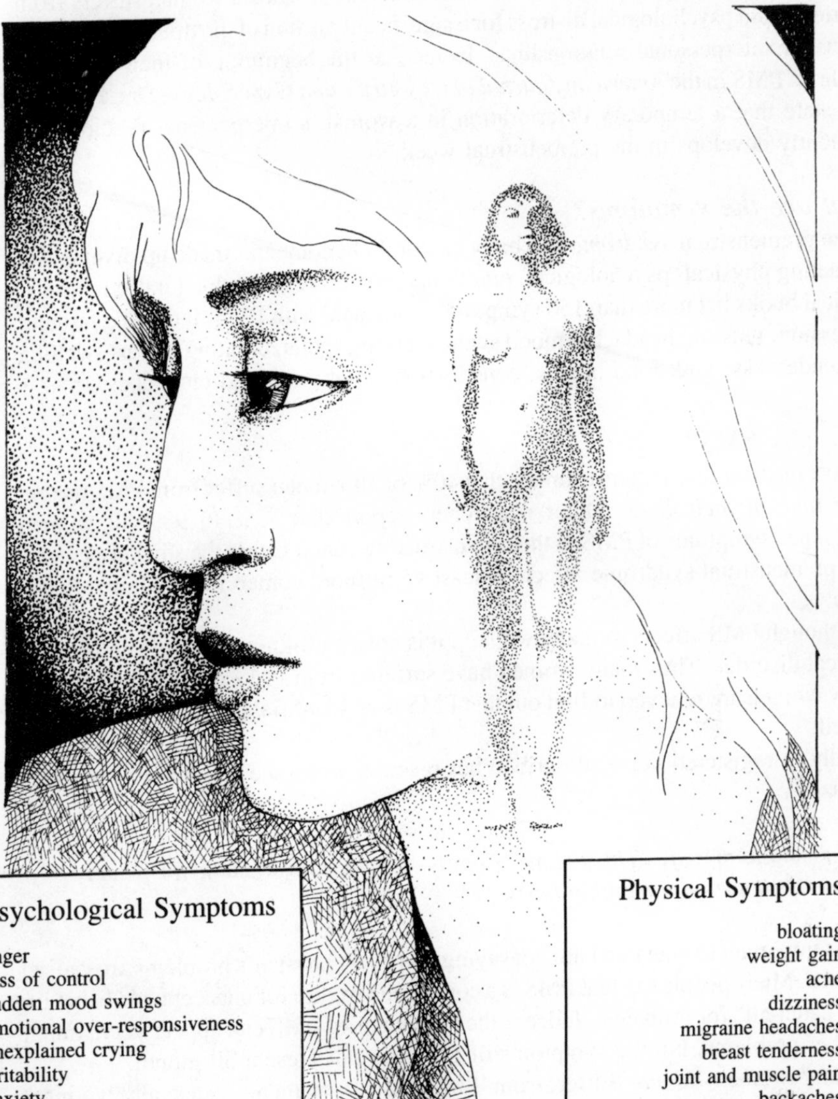

Psychological Symptoms

anger
loss of control
sudden mood swings
emotional over-responsiveness
unexplained crying
irritability
anxiety
forgetfulness
decreased concentration
confusion
withdrawal
rejection-sensitive
depression
nightmares
suicidal thoughts

Physical Symptoms

bloating
weight gain
acne
dizziness
migraine headaches
breast tenderness
joint and muscle pain
backaches
changes in sex drive
food cravings
constipation
diarrhea
sweating
shakiness
seizures

affect every aspect of a woman's life. Understandably, when a woman suffers from emotional and psychological distress for a significant portion of the time, it is going to affect her interpersonal relationships. In fact, at the beginning of their definitive article on PMS in the *American Journal of Obstetrics and Gynecology*, Drs. Reid and Yen state that a temporary deterioration in a woman's interpersonal relationships frequently develops in the premenstrual week.

What are the symptoms?

The premenstrual *syndrome* is a biobehavioral phenomenon made up diverse and interacting physical, psychological, emotional, cognitive and behavioral symptoms. Medical books list more than 150 symptoms associated with PMS, including fatigue, depression, tension, headache, mood swings, crying spells, bloating, breast swelling and tenderness, junk-food binges, constipation, joint pain, and clumsiness.

Who gets PMS?

Most medical researchers estimate that 40% of all women suffer from PMS *during some time in their lives*. Other researchers report that 85% to 90% of women experience symptoms of PMS in their menstruating years. Using the smaller percentage, premenstrual syndrome affects at least 45 million women in the United States alone.

Although PMS affects so many women, it is not a well-known or well-understood medical disorder. Thus many women have suffered from PMS without realizing it. Many women are relieved to find out that PMS is an identifiable problem that can be treated.

Sally, a registered nurse, described her reaction when she read about PMS in a magazine:

> *I said to myself, "This fits me. Finally, someone has a name for what I experience on a monthly basis."*

It is important to note that I am not saying that every woman's problems are caused by PMS. Many people say that PMS is a convenient excuse for unacceptable behavior or a "catch-all" for problems. Indeed, the symptoms of PMS can appear very similar to other problems, but the symptoms of PMS are not present all month.

Many women *do not* suffer from PMS. Many women—especially younger women—experience the time before their period as a creative time when they feel very sensitive to the world around them. If you fall into this category, you most likely do not need help now—although you might in the future. However, if you are suffering to such a degree that you think PMS is significantly interfering with your life, this book is for you.

Should I expect to get PMS?

If your mother or other women in your immediate family suffered from cyclical mood swings, irritability and depression, you may develop similar problems.

If you are going to develop PMS, it is most likely to affect you at specific times in your life, not during your entire lifetime. The time when you are most likely to be significantly affected by PMS is during your thirties. This is so common that PMS is often called "the midthirties syndrome."

Can I have PMS if . . .

. . . I'm nursing?
. . . I'm going through the change of life?
. . . I'm having erratic periods?
. . . I've had a hysterectomy?

The answer to all these questions is "yes." PMS is a cyclically related disorder, and a cyclical disorder can occur at any time during your life. Thus, contrary to popular ideas, the symptoms of PMS can be experienced by women who are *not* menstruating.

Are there tests that determine if I have PMS?

No. Contrary to what you might have read or what someone might have told you, the most current medical research clearly indicates that hormonal tests are inconclusive. There are no medical tests that can tell you if you have PMS.

How can I tell if I have PMS?

Charting is the only method that can tell you if you have PMS. Charting your symptoms shows you if there is a pattern to the changes occurring in your body.

Is PMS the same every month?

No, variation is the rule rather than the exception. If you have PMS, it is impossible to say that you will have the same set of symptoms every month and that your symptoms will last the same length of time.

The symptoms may start earlier than expected in some months and later in others. There are many variables that come into play: stress in your personal life or on the job, exercise, diet and so forth. These can speed up, delay or intensify PMS symptoms.

Some months are definitely worse than others. You may notice that one month is particularly difficult, and the next month is not nearly so bad. This can create a lot of confusion in your mind. Often, women report that about every third month is a particularly bad one.

Can I have PMS and still get menstrual cramps?

Yes. Many women have heard that if they experience cramps with their periods, they cannot have PMS. This is because of conflicting information about the relationship of menstrual cramps to PMS. However, my data, as well as the most recent medical research, clearly indicate that if you have menstrual cramps you have a greater tendency to suffer from PMS.[3]

Can PMS affect chronic physical disorders?

PMS can exacerbate several types of chronic disorders, including:

- Sinusitis
- Vaginal yeast infections
- Seizures
- Herpes
- Allergies
- Asthma attacks

In other words, if you have asthma attacks, you may have more asthma attacks when you are premenstrual. If you have seizures, you might notice an increase in the number of seizures before your periods. Dr. Dalton notes that no tissue in the body seems to be exempt from cyclical changes of the menstrual cycle, and all tissues can be affected by cyclical premenstrual symptoms or exacerbations of chronic disorders.[4]

Your doctor will not necessarily make the association between intensification of your chronic disorder and the fact that you are premenstrual. You can help your doctor make this connection by keeping track of your chronic illnesses in your charts.

If there's something physically wrong with me, why do I feel so bad emotionally?

We are used to separating mind and body. We think that if something is physical, it is not going to affect our mental attitude. But the mind and body are dynamically interrelated.

PMS is a physically based disorder that manifests itself physically, psychologically and behaviorally. The importance of understanding how PMS affects your attitudes and emotions cannot be overstated.

How do I know that the problems I'm having are related to PMS and not something else?

When a woman asks me this question (and almost every woman does), the problems to which she is referring are typically relationship problems: problems with her boyfriend, husband, children or friends.

This is the best way I have found to explain how PMS can both mix up (disrupt) and become mixed up with other things going on in your life. Look at a clear glass of water. This represents the relationship. Throw in a handful of sand. This represents PMS. What you get is murky water. Until you let the sand settle to the bottom, you will not see clearly which problems belong to the relationship and which belong to PMS.

Other problems or stresses that you might be experiencing should not be downplayed or scoffed at—either by you or your therapist. These might include other medical problems, financial problems, or problems at work. These problems can intensify PMS symptoms. If you are suffering from PMS, you will probably be less able to cope with these problems when you are premenstrual. They will seem more intense and less manageable during your PMS time. Conversely, once you begin to treat PMS symptoms, you will probably find that you are clearer about which problems are being caused by PMS and which ones are there for other reasons—but are intensified as a result of PMS.

Does it get worse as I get older?

Women whom I have counseled report that the symptoms seem to get worse as time goes by. They usually notice that the symptoms last longer and become more intense as they get older.

Does it ever go away or do I have to live with this for the rest of my life?

In many cases the symptoms can increase in intensity and duration until you go through menopause. However, treatments are available that include self-help measures and, if necessary, professional help. Self-help measures are explained in detail in the last chapter of this book. It will probably be a great relief for you to know that you can take action and do not have to spend your remaining years until menopause feeling like your life is a roller coaster.

CONCERNS WOMEN EXPRESS

A woman who visits the PMS Clinic is usually suffering from a number of different types of symptoms. These are the kinds of statements that I most frequently hear when a woman comes to me for counseling:

- *I feel so depressed.* I've got a good personal life, I like my job, and I'm fairly financially secure. Why am I so unhappy sometimes? There's no obvious reason. I can't figure it out.

- *I feel so confused.* I've been to several doctors, and they all tell me I'm fine. I know I'm fine for part of the month, but the other part of the month, I feel terrible. I'm confused because I don't know who I am at that time. I'm also confused because part of the time I love my family and the other time I feel like I can't stand them. It's like I'm on a merry-go-round.

• *I feel like crying.* Sometimes the whole world seems to be against me. Nobody understands me. Every time I turn to someone for help, it's a dead end. I'm afraid to get my hopes up for fear that I'll end up in tears again.

• *I feel so angry.* I'm angry because . . . well . . . I don't know why . . . I'm just angry. I'm angry a lot of the time just because nobody understands or believes me.

• *I feel embarrassed.* I'm embarrassed about my body. My face looks like I'm a teen-ager, and I'm 41. I'm bloated, and I look like I'm 3 months pregnant. It's embarrassing to feel this way even though everybody tells me I look OK. I'm also embarrassed about the commitments I make and sometimes don't keep.

• *I'm drinking a lot.* Drinking numbs me to what's going on. It helps me escape from the fact that I feel out of control sometimes. I drink to try to escape.

• *I crave sweets.* Normally I'm conscious about nutrition. I eat healthy foods, and I cook wholesome meals for my family. But during that part of the month, everything goes out the window, and I start craving sweets.

• *I can't stick to my diet.* Why is it that during part of the month I'm so good about eating the right foods, then all of a sudden it doesn't matter? I eat absolutely everything—and tons of it! I begin to binge on chocolates, carbohydrates and salty foods. I hate myself, but do I stop eating? No!

• *I feel helpless.* It's bewildering because I have spent so much time, energy and money trying to find out what's wrong with me. And nobody has come up with anything except expensive, inconclusive tests that don't tell me anything, much less make me feel better.

• *I can't cope.* Sometimes the most common everyday problems seem like insurmountable obstacles. Everyday things like getting out of bed and getting my kids to school seem as hard as climbing Mt. Everest! For no reason, the everyday things that are usually so manageable suddenly become impossible.

• *I feel crazy.* My emotions range from so happy and loving to so angry and hateful that sometimes even I can't believe it. I think that everyone thinks I'm nuts. I've heard of Dr. Jekyll and Mr. Hyde, but I never knew what this meant before. Now I do.

• *I can't cope with the torment in my mind.* If I could get rid of the psychological symptoms—the irritability, the rage, the depression—I would be willing to live with the physical part of it. I have suffered such mental distress that I have often wished that my doctor could find something physically wrong with me. At least then I would have an answer.

• *I feel ashamed.* My behavior can be so erratic and unpredictable. I attack my family verbally, and I'm insensitive to their feelings. Even though I know I shouldn't be doing it, my rage continues until I run out of energy. Then I'm ashamed of myself for hurting their feelings.

- *I feel like I've let my husband down.* Normally, my husband can count on me to be a contributing part of the family. But during those times of the month, I feel like I don't carry my share of the load. I think he's disappointed with me. I also think he's disappointed sexually. I can see why. I don't respond at that time. I wonder how much more of this he'll put up with.

- *I feel like a failure as a mother.* I worry about what I am doing to my children. I know that being a good mother means being consistent, and the last thing I am at that time of the month is consistent. I worry about the long-term effects of my behavior on my children.

- *I feel desperate.* I get to the point where I feel absolutely desperate. I feel that I've messed up everything—my life, my kid's life, my husband's life. I feel that they would all be better off without me. If I left, I would be doing all of us a favor.

- *I feel like a lot of my life has been wasted.* I have lived with these problems a long time. I've known how I've felt, but I never knew that there was anything that could be done about it. I've spent so much time searching for answers. Now I want to get on with my life. I'm tired of just existing, now I want to live.

Fortunately, after women have visited the PMS Clinic, I often hear:

- *Finally, someone understands.* It's really changed my life just to identify the problem. I've learned that I'm not alone, I'm not crazy, and—most important—there are solutions to my problems.

Take a Positive Approach

It is very important for you to go through a rebuilding process, to get to where you begin to like yourself again. But how depressing it can seem to have to rebuild or repair! Perhaps it makes sense to look at this process from another perspective: you have an excellent opportunity to start over again. Think of your past behavior as "water over the dam." Leaving your past behind is very valuable in regaining your self-control and self-esteem.

PMS IS COMMONLY MISDIAGNOSED AND MISTREATED

PMS is a recognized and legitimate medical problem. Yet it is neither well-known nor well-understood by the medical community. However, the *Journal of the American Medical Association* states: "Premenstrual syndrome (PMS) may be the newest women's health issue in the United States. Some severely affected women are now going public with their stories and are demanding treatment . . . from their physicians."[5]

Following is an explanation of the many reasons why PMS is so commonly misdiagnosed and mistreated. The different reasons are discussed separately, but they have overlapped across the years, creating myths and confusion.

Confusion about the Causes of PMS

PMS is a physically based disorder. Medical researchers do not agree as to the exact cause of PMS, but they agree that it is physical in origin. Medical researchers usually attribute its cause to endocrine abnormalities. Most believe that PMS is a hormonally based disorder that is the result of changes in the levels of one or two female sex hormones—progesterone and estrogen. It may be either a low level of progesterone or a ratio imbalance between progesterone and estrogen.

The most widely accepted theory is that a deficiency in progesterone occurs during the luteal phase of the menstrual cycle (the time between ovulation and menstruation). The most recent statement about PMS is that it can best be described as a state of brain activity that includes a set of different characteristics affecting mood, perception, thought, ideas, self-confidence and self-image.[6] The exact cause of PMS is still being debated among medical researchers, and new theories will surely continue to be put forth.

PMS is a Misnomer

Problems in the diagnosis of PMS can be attributed in part to its name. Some of the confusion about PMS has arisen as a result of how the syndrome was initially described and named by doctors. Unfortunately, the name "premenstrual syndrome" suggests that the condition occurs only prior to menstruation. However, menstruation does not have to be present for a woman to experience the cyclical occurrence of symptoms which comprise PMS. It can, for example, occur after a hysterectomy.

PMS can develop any time that your hormonal levels fluctuate. PMS patterns can occur in puberty or during menopause. This is because our bodies cycle hormonally whether we menstruate or not.

Often women who are involved heavily in sports do not menstruate, but suffer from PMS nonetheless. Additionally, if a woman is anorexic, she might suffer from PMS but fail to menstruate.[7]

A common misconception is that, if a woman has had a hysterectomy, she will not suffer from PMS. This is not true. If the uterus is removed but the ovaries are left intact following a hysterectomy (partial hysterectomy), the body will cycle hormonally just as it did prior to the operation. A partial hysterectomy does not exempt a woman from the possibility of having PMS. Many of the women I counsel who have had a hysterectomy report suffering from moderate to severe PMS.

Lack of Knowledge about the Female Body

Lack of knowledge about PMS in the medical community stems from the fact that, until recently, PMS was not addressed in most medical textbooks—including gynecology/obstetrics textbooks. Additionally, doctors typically study and are familiar with the "two M's"—menstruation and menopause.

With respect to the "first M"—menstruation—only in the last 10 years have menstrual cramps been determined to be physical in origin. Most doctors have finally stopped assuming and saying that menstrual cramps are "all in your head."

With respect to the "second M"—menopause—women in their early thirties who suffer from PMS frequently tell me they think they are going through an early menopause. The average age for menopause in the United States is 51.9 years. These women should not be expecting to be menopausal for another 15 to 20 years! The problem is that women are often unfamiliar with the workings of their own bodies. They have not had the opportunity to be educated about what happens to them between "M #1" and "M #2"!

Confusion of PMS with Psychiatric Disorders

PMS is commonly (mis)diagnosed as depression. In the *American Journal of Psychiatry*, Drs. Rubinow and Roy-Byrne point out that although PMS and emotional-psychiatric illness overlap, they are distinct medical disorders.[8] While the manifestations of PMS are often psychological, the origins are physical.

Nonetheless, much confusion still exists about the relationship of PMS to psychological disorders. Much of this confusion can be attributed to the fact that in the most commonly used medical reference handbook of mental illness, the *Diagnostic and Statistical Manual of Mental Disorders*, psychological symptoms of PMS match all the criteria for manic-depressive emotional disorders (with the exception of hallucinations). This manual is currently in the process of being revised, and the revisions will take into consideration the differences between PMS and emotional disorders such as manic-depression.

In the *American Journal of Obstetrics and Gynecology*, Drs. Reid and Yen note that "there is little to support the belief that psychological factors alone incite all other symptoms of the PMS."[9]

And *The Journal of American Medical Association* states: "The precise physiological mechanisms underlying the syndrome remain unclear . . . but its origins must be recognized as somatic, not psychological."[10]

In recent years, medical researchers have gathered evidence that the diagnosis of emotional illness often fails to account for the physical causes of the illness. One researcher, for example, reviewed 12 studies that included a total of 4,000 patients and concluded that 9% to 42% of the patients had physical problems at the root of their emotional illness.[11] These were unrecognized in the diagnosis of the problem.

Another study found that of 100 state hospital psychiatric patients, nearly half (46 percent) had an unrecognized physical illness that either caused or made worse the patient's emotional-mental state.[12] Thus the issue is not as simple as stating that PMS has not been treated. It has been *mis*treated under many different labels and categories: manic-depressive behavior, depression, schizophrenia, and in times gone by, hysteria.

Complexity of PMS

In the *American Journal of Obstetrics and Gynecology*, Drs. Reid and Yen suggest that the physical basis and underlying mechanism of PMS involves very complex neuroendocrine changes.

Endocrinology is one of the most complex fields of medicine. It is practiced by highly trained specialists who have yet to detect and understand all of the causes of hormonal imbalances.

The Usual Kinds of Medical Tests Do Not Help

Blood tests measure hormone levels at one point in time, but your hormone levels are always changing. Progesterone is periodically secreted into the bloodstream in spurts. This means that hormonal levels can change significantly every hour. With respect to PMS, what is important to determine is not your hormonal state at one point in time, but rather the pattern of hormonal change that is occurring in your body. Thus a blood test cannot capture the pattern of change in hormonal levels.

Picture it this way. A hormonal blood test is like taking a snapshot of a river that is always moving. The snapshot can only tell you about how the river looked at one moment in time. It cannot tell you about the constant change that is occurring in the river. With respect to PMS, what is crucial to determine is the *pattern of change*. Currently there are no proven biochemical tests that provide a complete picture of the functioning of endocrine pathways.[13]

Remember, hormonal tests are inconclusive. They are also very expensive. Charting your symptoms does not cost a penny and is the surest method to detect patterns of changes.

Take a Positive Approach

Take care of all of you! If you are suffering from PMS, it is crucial that you treat yourself with as much care and concern as you would treat someone else who had a medical problem and needed help.

CHAPTER 2

Do You Have PMS?

A Visit to the Clinic

KATHY'S STORY

It took me a long time to finally get myself some help. I tended to dismiss the idea that there was something wrong with me. After all, I'm a together person, I'm athletic, and I'm in good shape.

A friend started telling me about PMS. I half listened. I had heard about PMS, but it seemed like the most current fad on the talk shows and the latest "female problem" created by the women's magazines. I pretty much dismissed it as something to be taken seriously.

Then I got so depressed that I called a PMS clinic to see how much the treatment would cost. It seemed way too expensive. I didn't have much income at the time, and spending any of it on myself seemed like a luxury. If it weren't for my sister, I wouldn't have gone ahead and made an appointment. She told me how important she thought it was and offered to pay for my treatment.

I made an appointment, but then I started to feel better, so I canceled it. There didn't seem to be any reason to go to the clinic if I was feeling OK. Because I felt fine, the idea of spending money on myself made me feel guilty.

I made and canceled appointments a couple of more times. Each time I did I was convinced that I would feel "just fine from now on."

Then I got really depressed. This time I kept my appointment. It wasn't until later, after I began to understand my cycle, that I realized what I had been doing. I was making appointments when I was premenstrual and canceling them when I felt better!

COLLECTING THE FACTS

If you have been suffering from PMS, your life can seem confused and out of control. I invite you to "look into" a PMS clinic and be assured that you are not alone. "Listen" as other women relate their problems and ask questions.

In the exercises in this chapter, we are going to try to be as comprehensive as possible. I am going to ask you to carry out a self-report to determine three things: (1) your current symptoms; (2) when your symptoms started; and (3) your reproductive history over the past several years. The goal is to get the total picture.

Below is the self-report that each woman who comes to the PMS Clinic fills out. After you fill out the self-report, we will discuss how your responses compare with those of women who have come to the clinic for help.

PMS Self-Report

GENERAL INFORMATION

1. How old are you? ______________________________

2. What is your marital history (or history of intimate relationships)? ________

   ____

   ____

   ____

SYMPTOMS

3. What are the symptoms that you are experiencing that make you think you have PMS?

   a. Psychological symptoms? ______________________________

      ____

   b. Physical symptoms? ______________________________

      ____

4. What is the most problematic symptom for you?

   ____

   ____

5. Does there seem to be a pattern to your symptoms? __________ If so, what is it?

____

____

6. When did you realize there might be a pattern to your symptoms? ______

____

7. Who noticed that the symptoms might be cyclical? ______________

8. Do you think that over time the symptoms have increased, decreased, or stayed the same? ______________________________

TRIGGER TIMES

9. Note the time(s) when you think the symptoms became most problematic.

Physical Trigger Times	**Emotional Trigger Times**
Puberty ______________	Divorce ______________
Pregnancy ______________	Death ______________
Birth-control pill ______________	Other ______________
Tubal ligation ______________	
Abortion ______________	
Miscarriage ______________	
Hysterectomy ______________	

YOUR CYCLE

10. How long is your menstrual cycle? (Start counting the first day of your menstrual cycle as Day 1. The length of your menstrual cycle is the total number of days until the first day of your next cycle.)

____

11. Do you have menstrual cramps? ______________________

12. When do the symptoms that you experience go away? ______________

____

13. Describe your feelings when your period starts. ____________________

____

14. Describe how you feel following your period. ____________________

____

15. Is there a symptom-free period for you during the month? ____________

If so, how long does your symptom-free time last? ________________

____

16. Describe your *emotional* needs before and/or during your period.

____

____

____

PREGNANCIES

17. How many pregnancies have you had (including miscarriages and abortions)?

____

18. Did you experience toxemia during any pregnancy? ______________

19. Briefly describe what you experienced during the first 3 months of your pregnancy (pregnancies), and then describe how you felt during the last 6 months of your pregnancy (pregnancies).

____

____

____

____

CHILDBIRTH

20. How many living children do you have? ____________________

21. Have you ever had postpartum depression? __________________

    a. If so, after which birth? ________________________

b. How long did it last? ______________________

PROBLEMS

22. Have you been on birth-control pills at any time in your life? ________ If so, what was your reaction to them? ______________________

____

____

23. Have you ever had a tubal ligation? ________ If so, when? ________
24. Have you ever had a hysterectomy? If so, were your ovaries removed? ____
25. Do you experience monthly fluctuation in your weight? ________
    a. If so, what has been your highest adult weight (not including during pregnancy)? ______________________
    b. What has been your lowest adult weight? ______________________

FAMILY HISTORY

26. Do you think that your mother has/had PMS? ______________________
27. Do you think that your sister(s) has/have PMS? ______________________
28. Do you think that your daughter(s) has/have PMS? ______________________

SOCIAL RELATIONSHIPS

29. Do you think that the problems you are experiencing influence your relationships with other people? ______________________
    a. How have they affected your relationships with people closest to you?

    ____

    ____

    ____

b. How have they affected your other relationships (friends, neighbors, etc.)? ____

____

____

____

____

30. Do you think that the symptoms that you are experiencing affect your sex drive? __________ If so, in what way? ______________________________

____

31. Are there times when you are verbally abusive? __________ If so, describe these times. ______________________________________

____

____

____

32. Are there times when you are physically abusive? __________ If so, describe these times. ______________________________________

____

____

____

WORK LIFE

33. Do you think that the problems you are experiencing affect your work life? __________ If so, how? ______________________________

____

____

34. Consider the differences in your personal life and your professional life if you were not having ongoing problems with your cycle. ______________

____

____

____

MEDICAL HELP

35. Have you consulted anyone in the medical or mental-health fields about your problems? __________ If so, describe what they said and suggested to you.

____

____

36. Have you used any over-the-counter medications to relieve your symptoms? __________ If so, what are they? ______________________

____

____

DIET

37. How much caffeine (coffee, tea, colas) do you consume in an average day?

____

38. Do you drink alcoholic beverages? ______________________
    a. If so, how often? ______________________
    b. How many at one time? ______________________
    c. Do you drink at specific times? __________ If so, describe the pattern of alcohol use. ______________________

    ____

39. Does your tolerance for alcohol or other substances ever fluctuate? If so, when?

____

____

40. Do you eat breakfast? __________ If so, what do you eat? __________

____

____

41. Do you eat lunch? __________ If so, what do you eat? ______________

____

____

____

42. Do you eat dinner? __________ If so, what do you eat? ______________

____

____

____

HOW DO YOU COMPARE?

Below are compilations of 1,079 self-reports filled out by women who have been counseled at the PMS Clinic. These women clearly had symptoms that were bothersome enough that they felt they needed assistance. You can use these figures to see how you compare with women who have been diagnosed as having PMS after charting their menstrual cycles for at least 2 months.

- The average age of the woman who visits the PMS Clinic seeking help for her symptoms is 34.
- 42% of the women had been divorced at least one time. This figure is twice that of the national average. (For women in their thirties, the rate of divorce was higher, nearly 60%.)
- 57% reported that they were not the only ones to notice their symptoms.
- 83% reported that symptoms increased in intensity as they got older.
- 98%—practically all—reported "loss of control" as the most problematic issue.
- 54% reported that the trigger times for their symptoms were while using or after discontinuing use of birth-control pills, or after having been pregnant.
- 56% of women reported that their symptoms ended gradually each month, while 36% indicated that symptoms ended quickly with the onset of menstruation.
- 75% reported some sense of relief when their period started.

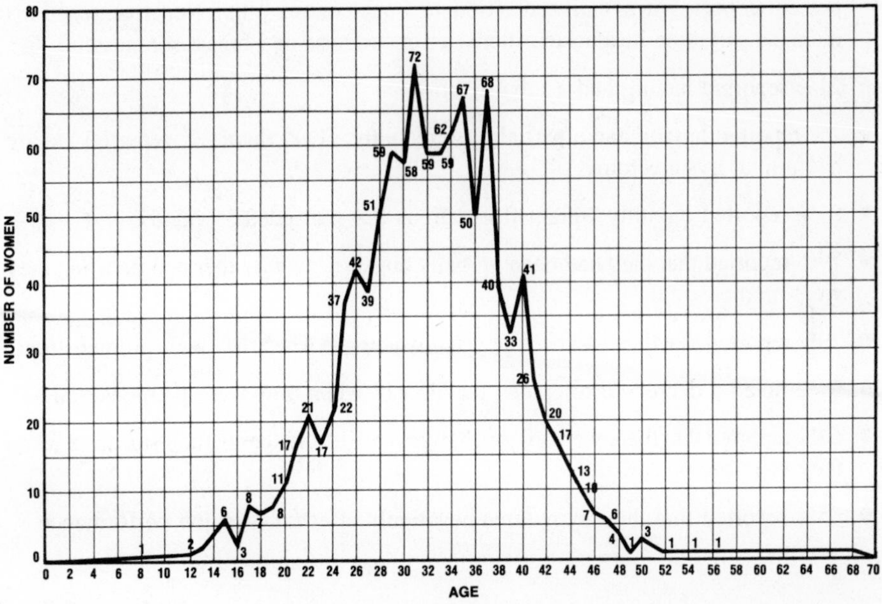

AGES OF WOMEN WHO VISIT THE PMS CLINIC
As this chart indicates, most women who visit the PMS Clinic are in their midthirties. PMS is often called "the midthirties syndrome" because this is the time when most women begin to notice problematic symptoms.

- 99% described themselves as more energetic and more positive in their outlook on life following their menstrual period.
- 57% reported that they experienced menstrual cramps on a regular basis.
- 60% had two or more pregnancies (including miscarriages and abortions). The same percentage had two or more living children.
- 15% reported that they experienced toxemia during pregnancy. (This is significant because Dr. Dalton states that 87% of women who have had toxemic pregnancies develop PMS at some time in life.)
- 64% reported that they had experienced postpartum depression that was more severe than the typical "baby blues" and that lasted more than 10 days.

- 87% reported that they had been on birth-control pills at some time. Sixty-six percent reported a negative reaction to birth-control pills. Negative reactions included migraine headaches, increased moodiness and breast soreness.
- 21% reported having had a tubal ligation.
- 7% reported having had a partial hysterectomy. (Less than .5% reported having had a total hysterectomy.)
- 81% reported monthly weight fluctuations that exceeded 5 pounds.
- 79% reported that they had been verbally abusive toward other people when they were premenstrual.
- 29% reported that they had been physically abusive when they were premenstrual.
- 57% noted a decreased tolerance for alcohol when they were premenstrual.
- 64% reported that there were major changes and differences in their sex drive when they were premenstrual.
- 85% reported that their symptoms negatively affected their job performance.

CORRECT DIAGNOSIS DEPENDS ON YOU

The most positive method to determine if you have PMS is the simple and inexpensive method of charting. Through charting, you can determine if there is a relationship between mood changes and the menstrual cycle.

You begin by collecting information about yourself: your moods, your physical state, your relationships. You determine not only when things happen, but also how intense they are when they happen.

If you chart your symptoms over a period of time that includes at least two or three menstrual cycles, you will most likely see a pattern. The pattern that you detect may or may not be related to PMS.

Charting consists of recording on a menstrual or frequency chart the dates of menstruation and the psychological/physical symptoms that occur at different times in the cycle. Ironically, expensive hormonal blood tests cannot accurately detect hormonal changes or imbalances. As mentioned before, charting—carried out by the woman herself—is the only accurate method.

My experience working with over 1,000 women is that PMS symptoms can be easily charted and accurately diagnosed after a 2- or 3-month period. Even if you are a young girl or an older woman, your symptoms can be charted.

Timing is the Key

PMS symptoms are related to monthly changes that occur in a woman's body. Menstruation is the external sign of this cyclical change. Symptoms cluster in relationship to the menstrual cycle. When you chart your symptoms each month, any relationship between your symptoms and your monthly cycle should become obvious.

The data that I have gathered on 1,079 women shows how, through careful and objective charting, you may discover that your symptoms vary in type, number and intensity from cycle to cycle. The key to correct diagnosis of PMS, however, is the *timing* of the symptoms. Correct diagnosis is *not* based on the type or variety of symptoms but rather *when* they occur in relation to the menstrual cycle.

YOUR DAILY CHART

A sample of several daily entries from one woman's chart begins on page 31. The daily chart is a day-to-day record of how you are feeling—both physically and psychologically. The pattern of changes in your state of mind and how you feel will become apparent after 2 to 3 months of daily charting.

Don't forget to chart on days when you feel great and are not experiencing any problems. In order for a pattern to be clearly established, *the good days must be charted along with the bad.*

Because the daily chart needs to be filled out over a 2- or 3-month period, we have provided you with three charts at the end of this book. Each one has space for 31 days. The charts begin on page 170. Fill in the actual date after the first day, second day, etc. of your charting. It doesn't matter what day of your cycle you begin charting. What is most important is that you begin charting as soon as possible.

Take a Positive Approach

The first step in regaining control is to accept responsibility for getting better. This means informing yourself about PMS—a process that you have already started. You also need to find out if you are going through physical and psychological changes on a regular basis and, if so, how these symptoms are affecting your life. You can do this by charting your symptoms. Taking responsibility for yourself in this way will begin to give you a sense of control.

✔ *Target Your Symptoms*

Focus on the most problematic symptoms that you are experiencing. Target four of these symptoms to chart daily. These should include two physical and two psychological symptoms. For example, two psychological symptoms that you might chart are irritability and depression. Two physical symptoms that you might chart are headaches and bloating.

Fill in the symptoms that you are going to chart:

Symptom #1
(Psychological) ______________________________

Symptom #2
(Psychological) ______________________________

Symptom #3
(Physical) ______________________________

Symptom #4
(Physical) ______________________________

✔ *Note Intensity of Symptoms*

Your symptoms should be rated on a scale of 0 to 10, with 0 representing least intensity of symptoms and 10 representing severest intensity. The number indicating the daily intensity of each symptom should be entered in the chart in the space provided after Symptom #1, Symptom #2, and so forth.

✔ *Note Menstruation/Ovulation*

The day that you start menstruating should be indicated by a circled "M." For each day that you have your period, indicate an "M." Also note the day that you ovulate. The day that you ovulate is usually the halfway point in your cycle. If you have a 28-day cycle, the halfway point is from the 13th to 15th days. You can tell when you ovulate because you will feel a little bit of cramping or pain in your lower abdomen, and your vaginal discharge will be heavier and have more mucus.

✔ *Watch What You Eat*

When you are charting, it is a good idea to record your intake of salt, sugar, caffeine and alcohol. If on a particular day you craved sweets or ate extra salty foods, for instance, this should be noted in the "Food Intake" section for that day.

✔ *Exercise*

Note what exercise you got for each day.

✔ *Comment on the Day*

The evening is the best time to reflect on the day's events. How did your symptoms affect your behavior? Were you less productive? Were you less able to cope with your children? Did you start an argument with your partner? If this was a good day, note the ways in which it was pleasant, productive and so forth.

✔ *Rate Each Day*

Finally, on a scale of 0 to 40, rate your overall mood for each day. In this rating, 0 represents a perfect day and 40 represents the worst possible day. A rating of 20 would represent an average day, neither very good nor very bad. (Note that if you were having a really bad day and *each of your symptoms* was rated at 10, this would add up to 40 for the day.)

Sample Daily Chart

Symptom #1 Irritability Symptom #3 Food Cravings
Symptom #2 Depression Symptom #4 Breast Soreness

Ratings: 0 (no symptoms), 1, 2, 3, 4, 5, 6, 7, 8, 9, 10 (most severe)

Month #1

1 Oct 1 (date) Symptom #1 0 Comments: ______
Symptom #2 0 ______
Symptom #3 0 ______
Symptom #4 0 ______
Food and beverage intake: Breakfast - good
Lunch - small
Dinner - good
______

Exercise: Jogged 2 miles
______

Comment on the day: Great

Overall rating for the day: 0

2 Oct 2 (date) Symptom #1 2 Comments: On edge with kids

Symptom #2 1

Symptom #3 1

Symptom #4 2 minor

Food and beverage intake: Breakfast - small
Lunch - good Dinner - good

Exercise: none

Comment on the day: Some irritability
in morning - mild.
all in all, a good day

Overall rating for the day: 6

3 Oct 3 (date) Symptom #1 2 Comments: Short fuse

Symptom #2 2

Symptom #3 2 Hungry for sweets

Symptom #4 4 Fairly noticeable

Food and beverage intake: Breakfast- small
Lunch - skipped Dinner - good

Exercise: none

Comment on the day: I've had better days

Overall rating for the day: 10

4 Oct.4 (date)
Symptom #1 4 Comments:
Symptom #2 2 Grey sky feeling
Symptom #3 2 Worked hard not to binge
Symptom #4 4

Food and beverage intake: Breakfast- small
Lunch - good Dinner - good

Exercise: Tried to jog but breasts hurt.

Comment on the day: Forgot a dental appointment — not a great day

Overall rating for the day: 12

Sample On-Sight Chart

Day #	Month #1	Month #2	Month #3
1	0000 = 0	0010 = 1	
2	2112 = 6	2110 = 4	
3	2224 = 10	3121 = 7	
4	4224 = 12	4232 = 11	
5	2224 = 10	4354 = 16	
6	4426 = 16	5576 = 23	
7	4446 = 18	5687 = 26	
8	6446 = 20	5698 = 28	
9	6646 = 22	7898 = 32	
10	8666 = 26	9889 = 34	
11	6866 = 26	10 10 10 10 = 40	
12	8886 = 30	9 10 9 10 = 38	
13	8888 = 32	Ⓜ 8621 = 17	
14	9899 = 35	Ⓜ 1001 = 2	
15	Ⓜ 6444 = 18	Ⓜ 1001 = 2	
16	Ⓜ 2112 = 6	Ⓜ 0000 = 0	
17	Ⓜ 0000 = 0	0000 = 0	
18	0000 = 0	0000 = 0	
19	0000 = 0	0000 = 0	
20	0000 = 0	0000 = 0	
21	0000 = 0	1000 = 1	
22	1000 = 1	0000 = 0	
23	0000 = 0	0000 = 0	
24	0000 = 0	0102 = 3	
25	0000 = 0	0101 = 2	
26	0000 = 0	5653 = 19	
27	1000 = 1	ⓞ 6662 = 20	
28	6642 = 18	3412 = 10	
29	ⓞ 4642 = 16	3212 = 8	
30	2412 = 9	1011 = 3	

YOUR ON-SIGHT CHART

This chart (see sample opposite) is to help you identify the pattern of changes in your monthly cycle. It contains the daily ratings you assign your symptoms on your daily charts. After 3 months of charting, the result is that "on sight" you will be able to identify clearly if you have a pattern of good times and bad times. The intensity of these times will also be apparent, as the rise and fall in the numbers refers to the rising and falling intensity of your symptoms. If you find that your symptoms do not have a clear pattern related to your menstrual cycle, you should consider discussing your symptoms with your doctor or a counselor.

✔ *Indicate Menstruation/Ovulation*

An On-Sight Chart is provided for you on page 232. To fill it in, refer back to your daily charts. Which day did you start your period? Transfer to the correct day on the on-sight chart the circled M that shows when your period started. What day did you ovulate? Transfer to the correct day on the on-sight chart the circled 0 that shows when you ovulated.

✔ *Indicate Intensity of Symptoms*

The coded numbers used in the daily chart that refer to the intensity of your symptoms should be entered into the on-sight chart. Add them up for each day, as indicated on the sample chart.

YOUR MOOD CHART

This chart (sample shown below) gives you a clear picture of your mood swings. It

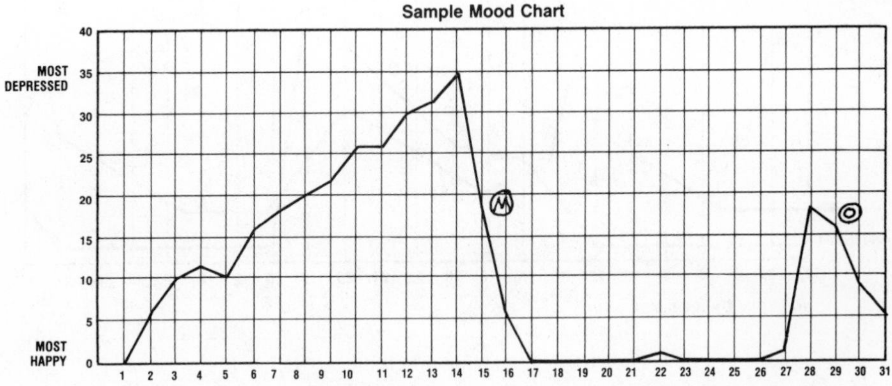

This sample chart is based on the numbers from Month #1 of "Sample On-Sight Chart."

is a graph on which you record your daily ratings, allowing you to see the pattern of emotional ups and downs that are associated with your menstrual cycle.

To make your mood chart, take your overall rating for each day from your daily chart and plot it on the blank graph provided on page 233. For each day, plot the overall rating, and then connect the points. If you feel ambitious, you can rate your moods for both the morning and the evening (as in the chart below). This way you can see how much your mood fluctuates within each day.

In the charts shown below, you will notice a general similar pattern of ups and downs for the menstrual cycle and the mood cycle. The first chart, *The Menstrual Cycle,* illustrates the changing levels of progesterone and estrogen during a typical cycle. When the pattern of progesterone change is compared to the second chart, *The Mood Cycle,* similarities are evident—particularly the dramatic changes that occur with the onset of menstruation. The second chart is the chart of one patient (out of 220) who participated in a study that was described in the *American Journal of Psychiatry.* Each participant was asked to rate her mood (depression and anxiety) twice a day for 3 months. The second chart is therefore carried out in almost the same way as is your Mood Chart, and its purpose is the same: it allows you to see the pattern of mood changes that you go through during your monthly cycle.

THE MENSTRUAL CYCLE

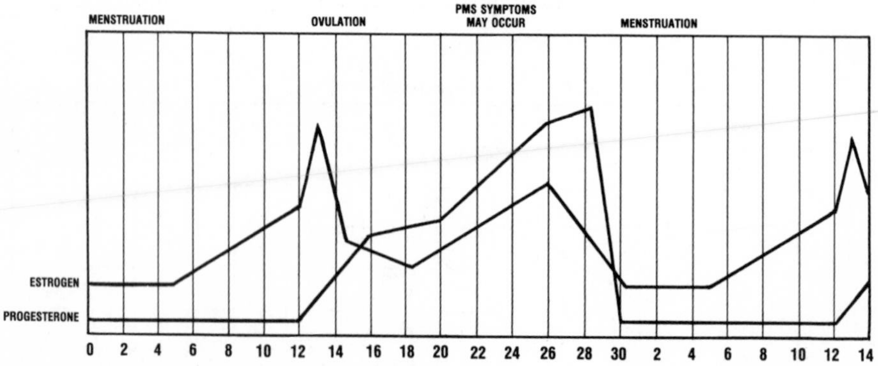

Reprinted with permission.[14]

THE MOOD CYCLE

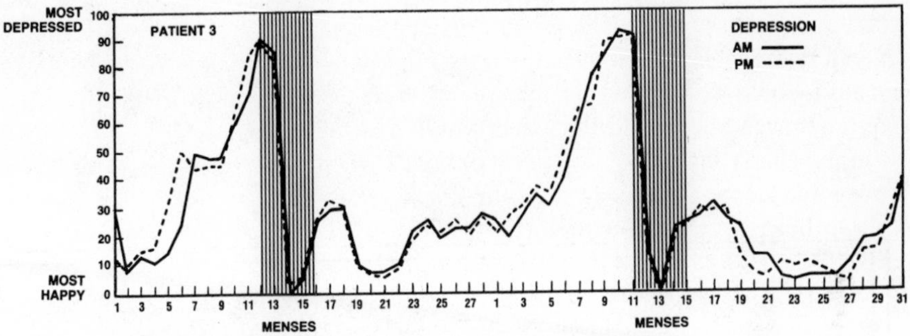

Reprinted with permission.[15]

Charting your symptoms is the first step in regaining control. Additional self-help measures are explained in the final chapter. You have taken action to deal with your problem, and this in itself is gratifying. Now your approach is active rather than reactive—you have the upper hand, rather than the problem controlling you. Good for you!

CHAPTER 3

PMS:
Unraveling the Syndrome

MARY'S STORY

Sometimes I am unable to do the simplest things. I frantically run around accomplishing absolutely nothing. I am a complete mess. One thing after another goes wrong. It's as if my nerves are stretched almost to the breaking point. I feel useless, worthless, and out of control. I am in a state of confusion. Making any kind of decision is out of the question. My mind doesn't seem to function properly. My thoughts rage between good and bad, right and wrong. I want to snap at someone and let all those built-up emotions erupt.

I know that's not the real me, so I sit fighting the anger within me. I want to be left alone with my madness so that later I won't regret something I said or did.

Then I become depressed. I cry without a reason. I feel I have nothing to live for, I feel totally worthless. No positive thoughts pass through my mind. Everything seems negative. I try to think of the good times, but even those feel sad.

I feel ugly and become self-conscious. My body feels oily and dirty and I can't seem to wash clean. My stomach and body swell, and my face breaks out, especially my chin. I become irritable and restless. I eat until I'm stuffed, and then I eat more. I become so tired that I can sleep sitting or even standing. I feel like a completely different person, like someone who is unpredictable. I don't know who I really am.

But when the blues fade away and I regain control of myself, I feel like I can tackle the world. I want to do everything at once because I feel so good, and I know these feelings won't last long.

I saw a psychologist who suggested I was depressed. Then I took a course about depression because I also thought depression was what was wrong with me. My symptoms were similar, but the treatment measures did not work for me when my PMS symptoms occurred.

I'm afraid to switch jobs to something more challenging because for days (sometimes weeks) I feel out of control. Also, I've noticed my self-confidence slipping away over the years. I keep thinking that, despite everything, there's still hope for me.

PMS: A COMPLICATED SYNDROME

You might not experience the same PMS symptoms that Mary describes above, or you might not experience your symptoms as intensely as she has. The intensity of her symptoms is quite common, however, and the extent to which she is suffering is not unusual for the woman who seeks help at the PMS Clinic.

In this chapter, we will talk about why it is important for you to understand the cyclical nature of your body's changes so you can begin to regain emotional and psychological control. We will explore:

- The pattern of thinking that most women go through in the process of uncovering PMS.
- How PMS affects women in different stages of life.
- Patterns and variations of PMS among women.

Emotional and psychological distress is almost always reported by women who suffer from moderate to severe PMS. When you come to an understanding of how your changes in moods and behavior are related to your body's cycle, you will begin to understand the pattern of your psychological symptoms.

There are a multitude of feelings that make up the premenstrual syndrome. Mary's story has touched on many of these. Let's unravel the syndrome so that we can begin to see how complex it is. Mary's feelings include the following:

I feel paralyzed.

My nerves are on edge.

I feel worthless.

I lack self-control.

I am confused.

I am unable to make decisions.

I am irritable.

I feel angry.

I want to withdraw.

I feel separated from myself.

I feel crazy.

I am afraid I will do something that I will regret later.

I feel depressed.

I cry uncontrollably.

My attitude is negative.

I have suicidal thoughts.

I am sad.

I feel ugly.

I feel self-conscious.

I feel tired.

I feel dirty.

I feel restless.

I am eating uncontrollably.

I sense that the "good time" is temporary.

Indeed, Mary is experiencing an entire syndrome made up of physical, emotional, psychological and behavioral symptoms.

UNCOVERING PMS: A PSYCHOLOGICAL PROCESS

The process of becoming aware of PMS is itself a psychological process with many ups and downs. This can make it difficult to trust your sense of what is happening to you, and it also makes it hard to get help. One minute you might feel confident, and the next you're questioning yourself.

If you are typical of other PMS sufferers, when you first become aware that PMS exists, you are quick to point out that you are "lucky not to be affected by it." You might say that you "have one or two bad days each month," and then add, "but of course this isn't PMS." In the process of finding out about PMS, you will probably move from this state of doubt and denial to one of active evaluation. You may not be clear about this transition. Rather, you will probably base your assessment on your intuition—an inkling or feeling that you have.

From Forgetting to Denial

Often the problem is that, if you are suffering from PMS, your body is changing so much during the month that you feel good for part of the month and bad for the rest of it. Your mental outlook is significantly different during the early and later parts of your cycle.

During the good time, you are likely to forget that you ever felt bad. And you probably also forget, or try to put out of your mind, your premenstrual behavior. You might be embarrassed about what you said or did. Often denial looks and sounds like forgetting, and can take place at the subconscious level.

From Denial to Self-Doubt

If you are typical of most women who suffer from PMS, you are likely to start second-guessing yourself. You wonder if your recollection of the bad time is accurate. You might think to yourself:

Maybe I'm exaggerating. Maybe I'm blowing this out of proportion.

The reason you doubt your recollections may be that you have learned not to trust yourself, not to trust your own judgment. This is a result of PMS itself: living with PMS over a period of time can strip away your self-confidence.

If you dwell on your premenstrual behavior, it is likely to make you feel anxious. Or, once you are feeling better and symptom-free, you may look back on last month and say:

I'm not sure it was really that bad. No, it wasn't that bad after all.

In other words, you mentally adjust your disconcerting thoughts. Unfortunately, you will probably be faced with many more months of bad times, and your symptoms are likely to increase in intensity and duration. You will probably find that your capacity for denial cannot keep pace with the accumulation of "incriminating evidence" that you gather about yourself.

From Self-Doubt to Relief

When you reach the point where your symptoms increase in intensity and your denial no longer makes sense, you will probably say to yourself:

Why is it that the sky appears blue to everyone but me? What's happening to me? Something is wrong. I know I'm not crazy.

At this point, you will most likely do a complete turnaround. Instead of maintaining that there is no problem, you will begin to think there is "definitely something wrong with me." You will probably admit to yourself that you sometimes feel horrible.

This can be a relief. What is happening is that your denial is starting to dissolve in the face of your own reality. This reality is evidenced by the following:

- How badly you feel.
- How negative you seem to yourself.
- How negatively you are responding to others.
- How negatively others are responding to you.

Actually, this is progress. Why? Because it means that the mental block that has prevented you from acting in your own behalf is now disappearing, thereby freeing you to start taking control of the problem.

From Relief to Active Evaluation

Once you hear about PMS and identify your symptoms, you are likely to find relief in the idea that you are suffering from a medical disorder. You will probably be grateful and relieved that someone has a name for what you are going through.

At this point, you might become angry because you have had to live with PMS for so long. Women are often bewildered to find that medical assistance has been available in Europe for many years.[16] They frequently ask me why women have not had opportunities to find out about PMS earlier—in school, for example, before the problems start.

Upon learning about PMS, my mother's response was one of sadness mixed with anger:

I never found the answer. It has been a two-sided coin to find out about PMS. I feel a sense of relief and happiness that you found something that works. But I'm angry that I had to go through it as many years as I did.

HOW PMS CAN AFFECT YOU AT DIFFERENT STAGES OF LIFE

Cycles of hormonal change occur in a woman's body during her entire lifetime. Each cycle involves significant hormonal fluctuations. Not every woman is affected by symptoms associated with cyclical change, but the majority of us are *at some time* during our lives.

I encourage you to observe the pattern—both physical and emotional—that takes place in your body:

- During your monthly cycle—from ovulation to menstruation.
- During pregnancy and afterwards—when your hormonal levels rise and fall significantly.
- Across your lifetime—from puberty through menopause.
- At times of stress—both mental and physical.

When a girl is going through puberty, significant changes occur in her body and in her mind. This can be an emotionally and psychologically stressful time. When she is in her twenties, she usually describes having one or two bad days a month. She might notice that she is becoming more emotional. Maureen, a musician in her late twenties, described it this way:

> *In the last couple of years, I've become this emotional being. I'm more sensitive to the world around me. Sometimes this is good and I feel more creative, and sometimes it means that I cry a lot more than I used to.*

When a woman is in her twenties, typically she does not feel incapacitated by the symptoms. When she reaches her thirties, however, the pattern of hormonal fluctuations in her body can change. As a result, the symptoms can increase in number and intensity. Without treatment, her symptoms can regularly interfere with her life until she goes through menopause.

Trigger Times

Times when your body fluctuates enough hormonally to trigger PMS symptoms include:

- During puberty
- After childbirth
- After a miscarriage

Take a Positive Approach

Pay attention to your body because, even though you feel great now, your body can change. You are better prepared if you realize ahead of time that these changes might occur.

- After a tubal ligation
- During or after discontinuing use of birth-control pills
- After an abortion
- After a hysterectomy
- During a divorce
- After a death

PMS: PATTERNS AND VARIATIONS

Even though there are typical patterns of PMS, there is also a great deal of variation from one woman to another, as well as a great deal of variation in each woman from one cycle to the next. Variations *between women* usually relate to which symptoms are present and how they are experienced. Variations *within one woman* usually relate to the intensity of the symptoms from day to day, month to month, and year to year. The variation in these patterns can leave you confused. Following are the cyclical variations commonly experienced by women with PMS:

- **Daily variation:** During the course of a single day, you can experience sudden mood swings, and feel waves of anxiety and depression.
- **Weekly variation:** The "2 good weeks/2 bad weeks" cycle, for example, means that your temperament can significantly fluctuate every 2 weeks. You might feel very low for 2 weeks and very high for the next 2 weeks.
- **Monthly variation:** Another dimension to the cyclical change associated with PMS is that you do not know exactly what to expect: each month can be different than the month before. If you chart your symptoms, you might notice that about every third or fourth month the symptoms are more intense.
- **Yearly variation:** As you get older, the frequency and intensity of the symptoms can increase. Thus the psychological burden can add up over the years. Each year can seem worse than the year before.

Elusive and Confusing Symptoms

PMS can also be confusing because so many *aspects* of PMS—especially the nature, intensity and timing of symptoms—vary significantly.

Even though there is a typical pattern of hormonal change, there is a great deal of variation in the *nature* of the symptoms from one woman to another. Writing in the *American Journal of Obstetrics and Gynecology*, Drs. Reid and Yen note that an individual's basic psychological makeup can affect how that person interprets the various aspects of PMS.[17] In other words, different women perceive and interpret their symptoms differently. How you interpret your symptoms has a lot to do with how you perceive yourself and what your life experiences have been.

The degree of intensity of the symptoms varies widely from woman to woman. Symptoms can range from mild to severe. For example, feelings of irritability can be mere short-temperedness or intense rage. Depression can range from crying for no reason to feeling almost indescribable, suicidal despair. A headache can be mild pain or an excruciating migraine. Anxiety can be felt as anxiousness or, in its extreme form, as panic attacks.

Diagnosis of PMS does not depend on the type of symptoms, but rather on the *timing* of the symptoms. With respect to timing, there are four typical patterns of PMS symptoms.

Patterns of PMS[18]

Pattern #1	Symptoms appear 2 to 10 days prior to the onset of menstruation and continue for up to 24 hours after the period begins.
Pattern #2	Symptoms appear at ovulation (usually 13 to 15 days prior to the onset of menstruation), continue for a few days and subside for 2 to 5 days. Symptoms then recur and continue for up to 24 hours after the period begins.
Pattern #3	Symptoms begin at ovulation and last approximately 2 weeks or up to 24 hours after the period begins.
Pattern #4	Symptoms begin at ovulation and continue for 3 weeks until near the end of the menstrual period.

With respect to your own pattern, keep in mind that you do not always ovulate on the same day in your cycle. Even if your period is exactly the same length of days each cycle, the day that you ovulate can vary. This can affect the timing of your symptoms.

Your state of mind and what is happening around you can also affect the timing and onset of your symptoms. If you are worried about becoming pregnant or losing your job, just to name two examples, this can delay your period for many days or weeks. When this happens, there can be a tremendous buildup of anxiety and tension. Your symptoms will typically be felt more intensely during these times.

The Cloud Lifts: This Can Vary Too

Everyone who suffers from PMS gets some relief from the symptoms some of the time! But exactly when the relief comes varies from one woman to the next. Many women agree with Jeanne's comment:

The day I get my period, the cloud begins to lift.

Others note that they aren't rid of their symptoms until they are halfway through or finished with a period. This is also common. Remember, with PMS, *variation is the rule rather than the exception.*

Almost invariably, when I ask women who come to the PMS Clinic how they feel when their period starts, they answer:

I have more energy.

I'm more optimistic.

I'm cheerful.

I get things done.

I like my family.

I like myself.

The overwhelming majority say that they get relief and a new outlook on life. Even if the cloud does not lift completely, a woman knows relief is on the way. Some women feel positively euphoric once their period starts.

CHAPTER 4

The Vicious Cycle:
Anger/Guilt/Denial

NANCY'S STORY

Let's say I have errands to run. I ask my family: "Please have the kitchen cleaned up before I get back."

It sounds reasonable enough. But when I get back, the dishes aren't done, and everyone's watching TV. No one bothers to offer an excuse. The scene is set for World War III to start.

"I can't believe the dishes aren't done!" I say.

Then my voice goes up a couple of notches. "I can't believe that you're all just sitting around watching TV. No one ever does anything they say they're going to do! I'm sick of this!"

At this point, I become very much aware of myself. I think to myself: "I shouldn't be getting so angry."

It seems like I'm outside myself, watching myself. It's strange. I wish I could stop. But I can't. Actually, I just keep getting angrier.

"Get up this instant! I'm sick and tired of doing all the work around here. Get in there and do the dishes. Clean up your mess in the bathroom, too!" By now, I'm yelling.

I'll continue in this vein, getting angrier and angrier, louder and louder, until I run out of energy. I may add something else like, "I'm sick of doing everything. You never help me."

This last line is delivered with near-explosive force, as I glare at my husband and run out the back door—slamming it, of course.

Once I'm outside, I break down crying, and I can't stop. I cry until

> *I can't cry anymore—until I'm mentally and physically exhausted. Then I start to feel guilty about what I've just done.*
>
> *After getting in the car and driving around for a while or sitting in a kind of daze, I finally get it together again and go back to my family. I say something like, "I probably shouldn't have exploded. I'm sorry."*
>
> *My family is relieved that I'm back and speaking to them again. But I don't feel any better. I go over everything again and again in my mind: "Why did I do that? Why did I say that?"*
>
> *Then I think: "I'm a failure as a mother. I'm a lousy wife. My family would be better off without me."*

LOSS OF SELF-CONTROL

Does the foregoing scenario strike a familiar chord? When I go through this scenario with women, they usually say, "It sounds like you've got a crystal ball."

Why? Because I've been there too.

Thinking about Nancy's story will help you realize that you are not alone; many women report a similar type of blowup. Although your premenstrual behavior may seem to you to be strange, weird, or crazy, this kind of angry outburst is shared by millions of perfectly normal, perfectly sane women!

Women tell me that they feel *out of control,* and *confused* or *angry* with themselves. They describe the progression of their anger as moving from (1) a sudden loss of a sense of humor to (2) an angry outburst to (3) verbal abuse to (4) guilt, depression, and—sometimes—desperation. My own work and other studies have shown that, in severe cases of PMS, the depressed and angry state of mind of a premenstrual woman can have unfortunate consequences such as child abuse and suicide attempts.

The experience of being *out of control* is one in which you lose your will to act and your power to control your actions. First comes confusion about what you want. Then, even if you make up your mind to do one thing, you are likely to find yourself doing something quite different. You seem to be two persons. Women describe the feeling of losing control in different ways:

> *Someone else takes over.*
>
> *The devil moves in.*
>
> *I'm not me.*

Being *in control* of yourself means being able to exercise a directing influence over yourself. It means that you can make up your mind, and then carry out your plan.

In this chapter, we will talk about the psychological and behavioral patterns that typically develop with PMS. We will also talk about how you can feel crazy and guilty a lot of the time. Then we will discuss how different symptoms can interact, compound, and lead to low self-esteem and depression. Finally, we will analyze this process more fully and look at how your body and mind interact with your social environment.

ANGER

When you become angry and blow up, you may feel that part of you has separated from the real you and is acting out of control—differently than the way you normally act.

One part of you says, "Stop! You're going to regret this." The other part continues with the rage. Often, you will not be able to stop yourself. Sally, 34, a dental assistant, described how this happens:

> *I could feel the anger building up in my body. It seemed to have a mind of its own. It felt like I was going to explode.*

When you stop and reflect upon your actions, you may conclude that you are crazy because you are "acting like a lunatic." As a result (especially if this has happened more than once), you may not trust yourself to open your mouth in public, lest that other person inside come spewing out!

The Separating Phenomenon

The time when you are most likely to feel separated from yourself is precisely when you become very angry and have a blowup. I call this the *separating phenomenon.*

The separating phenomenon is the experience of sensing yourself as two different individuals. One feels like a person who is inside you acting out what you feel emotionally. The other feels like a person who is outside you observing your behavior in a detached way. This can be confusing. As Claire said to me:

> *I get to the point where I wonder who the real me is. I mean, which emotional person am I anyway?*

There is a dimension of self-consciousness about the separating phenomenon. At the very moment when you are criticizing your husband or yelling at your kids, you are also probably asking yourself in a very calm fashion:

> *What am I doing? Why am I exploding this way? He only spilled a glass of water. This is bizarre.*

The sense of separating from yourself, strange as it may seem, is quite common among women who suffer from PMS. Many of my patients talk about being "out of control" and "feeling crazy" in the same breath. These two feelings are closely related, and they can lead to loss of self-esteem.

Setting Up for Failure

With PMS, you are very likely to have emotional extremes in your life each month. At one end of the spectrum are angry outbursts and blowups. At the other end are guilt and depression. These extremes are closely connected: having an angry outburst leaves you feeling guilty about the incident. So when you are symptom-free, you might say to yourself:

> *That was ridiculous. That was the last straw! I won't do that ever again.*

In other words, you make a contract with yourself that says you will not do next month what you did this month. In the process, you convince yourself of your ability to maintain control next month.

This is the first step of what I call the *vicious cycle*—the anger/guilt/denial cycle. What are you doing? Unknowingly, you are setting yourself up for failure.

Next month comes. For reasons beyond your knowledge and control, you are unable to keep the contract that you made with yourself. You become angry, and it happens again. You blow up. Only now the problem is compounded because frustration is added to your anger. You made a promise you failed to keep. In addition to the angry outburst, you probably feel defeated and ineffective. You probably get angry with yourself and think:

> *I can't believe that I can't keep a promise to myself for even one single month.*

You may wonder, "What kind of person am I anyway?"

Many women carry their criticisms even further and say, "I'm a worthless person."

GUILT

The guilt starts when you begin to blame yourself for your premenstrual behavior. You might say to yourself, "I should be more in control," and you mentally punish yourself for being out of control. You allow yourself no room for mistakes, no breathing space. This is the buildup of the first layer of guilt.

Nancy's story at the beginning of the chapter will help you see how the guilt starts. Refer back to it and review it for a moment. What happens after Nancy flies into a rage and leaves the house? She returns to talk to her family. When she does, her family is usually fairly understanding. They are willing to forgive and forget. The problem is that *she* is not able to forgive and forget. Her behavior is not OK with her. She keeps that guilt alive, even nurses it by feeding it with self-recriminations.

The inability to control the situation—the anger and the guilt—can be the most debilitating part of PMS. If you are like many other women suffering from PMS, you would prefer to deal with the tangibles of the body rather than these intangibles of the mind. Unfortunately, the physical and mental aspects of PMS are inseparable. They come in the same package.

DENIAL

Later, thinking about your angry outburst, you probably say to yourself, "I can't believe it." Then you decide, "That wasn't me." But consider for a moment what it means to say "That wasn't me." It is the same as saying, "I'm not me." A statement like this suggests a sense of separation and estrangement from who you are, from your self.

Denial is a big part of PMS. Denial starts when you are feeling symptom-free and you look back on last month and say to yourself, "That wasn't me," and "That can't happen again."

It is important to point out that each of us tends to deny some of our behavior some of the time. Why? We want to be in control. To a certain extent, this type of thinking is crucial to a healthy sense of self. Too much denial, however, is unhealthy because it means that we are out of touch with what is happening. As Linda said to me:

> *You do your best to deny the symptoms, but eventually you have to accept them because they keep coming back.*

Upping the Ante

When you actively deny your PMS symptoms, you are like Nancy, the woman in the story at the beginning of the chapter. You promise to "get this thing under control next month." You are determined to use your willpower to avoid another bad month. Typically, you say to yourself:

> *Now that I'm in control, I feel so much better. I won't lose it again.*

Your "proof" that you will be in control next month is that your body feels fine right now, and your state of mind is so positive.

You should be congratulated for your determination, but I must warn you that you are upping the ante for next month when—through no fault of your own—you will most likely lose the next round.

It's Not Simply "Mind Over Matter"

When you promise yourself that you are not going to allow your premenstrual behavior to recur, you are trying to exert the power of your mind—your willpower—over a physical condition. But if you suffer from PMS, making up your mind during the good times will not change the chemistry of your body during the bad times.

What is actually happening when you say to yourself, "As long as I know this happens every month, then next month I can control it and keep it from happening again"? You are trying to assert your willpower over the chemicals in your body. This may include promising yourself to stick to that diet, promising your husband or boyfriend that you will not blow up again, or convincing yourself that everything is really OK and that you will not cry again for no reason. However, the usual things do not and cannot work.

You will come to appreciate the futility of trying to control PMS with your mind alone. Does it make sense for someone who has diabetes to get angry and say: "I am going to control diabetes by asserting my mind over my body. I'm not going to take my insulin because I can control diabetes with my mind." Although PMS may not seem to you as physically based as diabetes, it is. Don't blame yourself for having a physical problem. Rather, give yourself credit for your determination and perseverance in finding help.

You Must Act on What You Know

Even when you are well-informed about the multifaceted nature of PMS, your knowledge about PMS cannot prevent the symptoms of PMS—symptoms such as bloating, irritability and depression—from flaring up. You may be able to identify clearly your physical symptoms, such as migraines and backaches, but you might still attribute your anxious and depressed state of mind to everything *but* a physical disorder. Keep in mind that:

- Your knowledge alone cannot overcome a chemical imbalance in your body.
- Your willpower alone cannot overcome a chemical imbalance in your body.

However, being well educated about your problem will certainly help! Your knowledge and your willpower are crucial ingredients in getting better. They are the first steps in regaining control. But you must also act on what you know in order to get better.

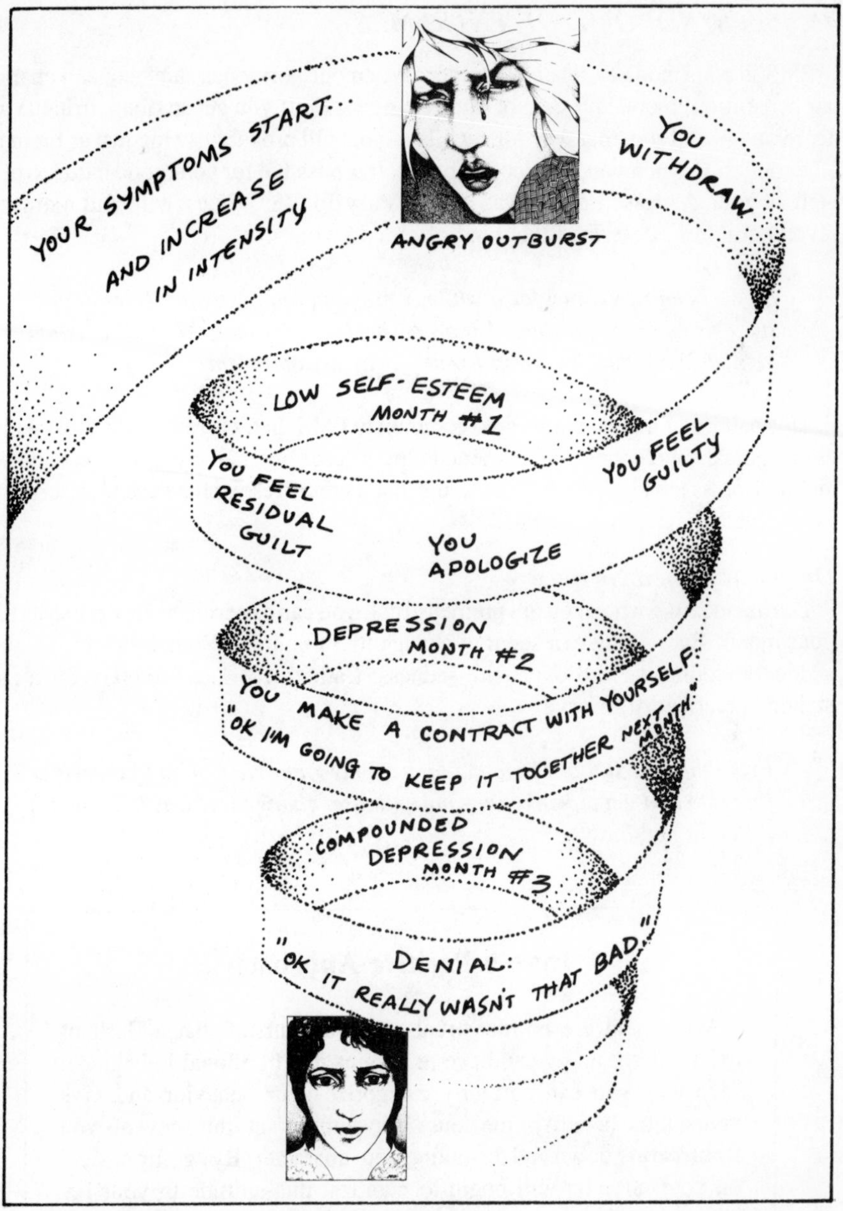

SETTING UP FOR FAILURE: THE VICIOUS CYCLE

PMS: A SYNDROME OF EXTREMES

PMS is a hormonally related disorder. When our hormones fluctuate and change, our perception, mood and state of mind change also. If you get anxious, irritable and depressed—and stay that way for a while—you will probably swing just as far in the other direction when you start feeling better. It is possible for your good mood to be as high as your depressed mood was down. Mary Jo, 48, a housewife and mother of several children, described this kind of mood swing:

> *If I've been way down for a while, I'm going to go way up. I dread one stage as much as the other. I know my husband does too. When I'm flying high, I know that he doesn't really trust my optimism.*

This pattern of mood swings is so common to PMS that, currently, the most widely used medical source for defining mental illness describes manic-depression (a bipolar mood disorder) in almost the same terms that medical researchers use to describe the psychological symptoms of PMS.

Dramatic Mood Swings

During the time when you are premenstrual, you can experience very rapid shifts in your mood. Everything can seem to change in 5 minutes. Women talk to me about suddenly feeling washed over with sadness. Catherine, 31, a secretary for a radio station, described it this way:

> *From the time it took me to get up from my typewriter to go to the water fountain and get a drink, my whole mindset changed. It was like I was a different person.*

Take a Positive Approach

When you are premenstrual, remind yourself that a flash of irritability or anger can have its origins in a hormonal imbalance. This way you can correctly categorize your behavior and give yourself the benefit of the doubt. Most important, this prevents you from tearing down and devaluing your character. By "going easier" on yourself, you will begin to manifest this attitude in your behavior toward other people. You will also begin to give them the appropriate cues as to how they can best support you.

It is as if we must fight to maintain a sense of balance. Catherine also described another incident, one that is not unusual for the woman who suffers from PMS:

> *I had to cling to self-control. I had to fight the impulse—what seemed like an uncontrollable impulse—to cry in the grocery store.*

Changes as rapid as this are very confusing. Even more confusing is that when we finally begin to see a pattern, it changes.

Mental Roller Coasters

Confused thinking can result from feeling emotionally off balance during a significant period of time. This symptom of PMS is described as "cognitive indecision" and means that your thinking becomes quite confused and fuzzy when you are premenstrual. As Diane, 34, a head nurse in a hospital nursery, said:

> *I have moments of clarity, but these are few and far between. More and more often, it's like I'm in a daze. I don't know how I manage to get through the day sometimes.*

Decreased concentration, indecision, and paranoia are other dimensions of the cognitive aspect of PMS. This was described by Sue, 33, a security worker:

> *It's like I have a reality problem. I don't remember really important things. Then, after a while, I don't know what is important or what has priority. I'm late a lot of the time for appointments and commitments, or I just don't show up.*

When your thinking is confused and dazed for a significant portion of the time, it is difficult to make plans or see them through. When you are on an emotional roller coaster, understandably your thinking process is affected. It is difficult to focus and concentrate on projects. Kathy, a legal assistant for a large law firm, described it this way:

> *I would begin projects—I mean five or six different projects—and none of them would ever get finished. A year ago, I started painting the living room. Six months later, the room was only half painted. There were about four other projects around the house that were in the same state of confusion. I swear I never used to be this way.*

A real problem with this symptom is that it prevents us from getting help for ourselves because we can feel so indecisive. If we do ask for help, sometimes it is impossible for us to state clearly what we need due to an inability to focus our thoughts. Additionally, we might be very sensitive to rejection (another symptom of PMS) and therefore have difficulty accepting help.

Dramatic mood swings that occur again and again can leave you mentally devastated. If you do not understand what is happening to you on a regular basis, it is understandable that you might begin to question your sanity.

LOSS OF SELF-ESTEEM AND DEPRESSION

The anxious/depressed state of mind that is typically a part of PMS can result in a feeling of worthlessness. You can feel as though you cannot handle things, make decisions or carry through with decisions at certain times of the month. These insecure and negative feelings can add up, compound, and become more intense over time.

After going through the anger/guilt/denial cycle many times, you can learn not to like yourself. Your sense of self diminishes, and your self-image is likely to become quite negative. You probably feel that you are losing your self-respect and your sense of being in control of your life. It is crucial for you to understand that you have a physical disorder, and your low self-esteem most likely stems from this.

Compounded Depression

If you suffer from moderate to severe PMS, you regularly go through a psychologically debilitating process. The problem increases cumulatively. The burden of one month is added to that of the month before, and the burden of one year is added to that of the year before.

When anxiety and depression are compounded, they tend to create a fearful, anxious, and depressed attitude toward everyday life. Karen, 33, a dental technician, reported:

> *When you have a good day, you don't know how long it will last.*

Consciously or subconsciously, you can begin to fear your own body. You might feel trapped and resentful, and think that it's not fair that your body is doing this to you.

Depression Hangovers

With PMS, the separate symptoms interact—one sets off and aggravates another. Similarly, the good times and bad times are related—one significantly influences the other. During the bad times, you may create problems for yourself and others. The resulting frustration and guilt can "hang over" into the good times. The good times are therefore more like a residual stage of PMS, rather than a time when you feel good about yourself.

During the good times, you probably try to make up for the problems you've created. Carol, 39, a mother of two and an elementary-school teacher, told me:

> *During the good time of the month, I try to undo what I've done during the bad time of the month.*

This may mean that you try to do more than is humanly possible! You overextend your emotions, your hospitality, and your patience beyond the point that you normally would.

Ultimately, it may seem that you are on a treadmill, trying to get ahead of the problem. Despite your efforts, however, you keep falling back into a slump. Your guilt, anxiety, frustration, anger and resentment may pervade most of your days. As a result, you can feel ill at ease most of the time. You might feel as though you have no time when you feel truly calm, guilt-free, and at peace with yourself.

Desperate Depression

PMS often increases in severity as you get older. There seems to be no respite. As Joanne, 44, a divorced mother of three, said:

> *For me, it's like there's no tomorrow. There is only today. And what I know about today is that it is unbearable. I don't feel like being alive if this is what it's like.*

Asked to describe what this buildup of depression over the years feels like, Joanne said:

> *Desperate depression, that's what it is. I'm a failure as a mother. My family would be better off without me.*

Suicidal thoughts, unfortunately, are a fairly common symptom for women who have been suffering from PMS for a long time. In a typical week at the PMS Clinic, I counsel two or three women who report being suicidal.

Having suicidal thoughts does not necessarily mean that you are going to attempt suicide. Generally, thoughts of suicide are a form of denial and a desire to escape. But if you have suicidal thoughts, don't ignore them. Look at them as an indicator. You need to pay attention to what is happening to you and get some assistance.

REGAINING CONTROL

If you have suffered from PMS for a long time, you are probably no longer accustomed to being in control for part of the month. The problems have been big ones. Many patterns of thought have developed around your behavior. It is time to stop berating yourself. Whatever you can do to realize that your past behavior is behind you is very valuable in regaining your self-control.

When I counsel women at the PMS Clinic about the anger/guilt/denial cycle, I ask them to carry out the self-help exercise on the opposite page. I also want you to do this exercise so you can associate that out-of-control feeling with PMS. You will probably have a very clear mental picture of the times when you lost control. When asked about her experiences, Patricia, 35, a small-business owner, said:

> *Oh yes, that was the time when I came unglued and the mushroom cloud went up!*

You are not likely to forget situations in which you felt intensely emotional. In fact, you probably often recall your blowups and use them as ammunition against yourself.

Make the Connections

There are two reasons for going through this exercise. First, you need to connect your past behavior with the fact that you are suffering from a medical problem. Second, you need to understand fully that this is not your fault (or anybody else's). You should try to get to a point where you can clearly see the connections and associations between your behavior and your PMS. I ask you to remember the big blowups so you can begin to understand that PMS was a major ingredient in that argument, disagreement or flare-up. When you begin to associate the bad times with PMS, you can start to give yourself some breathing room. You can take a deep breath and say:

> *Wow, I think PMS has played a big part in my anger and guilt and has been a major reason for my low self-esteem.*

Associating the angry blowups with PMS hardly excuses your behavior or resolves the confusion that has probably arisen with your family and friends. But it gives you permission to stop berating yourself and permission to forgive yourself. When you make the connection between the blowups and what is happening in your body, you can forgive yourself for events that have already taken place. The events of the past need to be forgotten so that you can move to more positive things.

It might help to compare PMS and diabetes. If you found out that you had diabetes, you would hardly blame yourself. Diabetes is a physical disorder with symptoms

Self-Help Exercise

TIME OUT: CLEAR THE DECKS

1. Set aside a block of time for yourself. Make sure the kids are being watched. Hire a babysitter if necessary. Take your phone off the hook. Lock the door. Give yourself permission to do this, and tell yourself that you are taking steps to help you *and* your loved ones.
2. Begin to think about those incidences when you lost control and were on the verge of leaving your husband, getting a divorce, quitting your job, etc. Dredge up the uncomfortable memories—the big ones—and think about how you felt during those times.
3. Try to remember the progression of your anger. What form did that out-of-control feeling take? Sullenness, impatience, inability to cope, hostility, aggression, verbal abusiveness? Did you throw a vase at your husband? Did you hit your child?
4. Reconstruct the scenes again and try to remember where you were in your menstrual cycle. Does it seem that your period started soon after the incident occurred? It is important for you to at least estimate the timing with relation to your cycle. You need to establish the fact for yourself that you may act out of control during part of the month (premenstrual), but deal very calmly and rationally with the same conditions during the other part of the month (non-premenstrual).

similar to PMS. If a diabetic is not stabilized, episodes of irritability, problems with mental function and lack of physical coordination can occur. Diabetes is a disease that everyone recognizes as a medical problem. You should begin to think of PMS in the same way.

SELF-ESTEEM AND MIND/BODY/SOCIAL INTERACTIONS

Most women intuitively perceive the relationship of their body and mind to their social environment. This relationship shows up very clearly when I ask women, "How do you think your life would be different if you didn't have PMS?" Alice, 36, a data analyst, fully captured the whole dynamic when she reported:

> *I think that I would be a lot more successful. I'd be a better mother. I'd be a better wife. I'd be a better friend. I'd be better at my job. I'd be better all*

around. But what happens now is that I start getting these little bits and pieces together and then this stuff comes and scatters it all around. Then I've got to go and pick up all the pieces again. Sometimes I feel good, and I think to myself, "OK, good, let's go! I'm ready to get organized and moving." Then a few days (sometimes even a few hours) later, everything fizzles. All my energy is gone. I begin to feel like a lousy mother, wife and friend. I lose my sense of direction, and my work suffers. Sometimes, I can't figure out who I am or if I'm anybody.

Self-esteem has physical, social and psychological components because intellectual, emotional and bodily processes occur simultaneously. Although they may be discussed and described separately, they are always inextricably entwined. Let's see how this works.

From the Inside Out

The physical changes that take place every month in your body can directly affect your mood. This influences your behavior, thus affecting the people around you.

Let me give you a quick example of the physical-psychological-social dynamic of PMS. When you are premenstrual, your blood-sugar level can drop precipitously

---

Self-Help Exercise

YOU DESERVE A BREAK!

1. Give yourself a break! Promise yourself that there will be no more guilt and no more recriminations.
2. If you have been berating yourself, now is the time to go to the other extreme and pamper yourself. If you have trouble doing this, think about how easy it has been to punish yourself—an extreme. Now think about how you must balance out that extreme with another: kindness, patience, and generosity with yourself. For example, if you like to read, go to the bookstore and browse. Or, you might take a long, hot bath. Or, how about taking an early-morning walk before anyone in your family gets up?
3. Make a list of the things that you have done to help others that you would like to do now for yourself.

---

low. This can cause an anxiety attack in which you feel scared and withdraw. Or, it can cause you to be hostile, argumentative and aggressive. Either reaction—withdrawal or aggressiveness—is going to affect the people around you. Your behavior can make them respond in an anxious or hostile manner. This, in turn, can make you even more anxious or aggressive. Over time, this type of interaction can lead your social interactions in a downward spiral, ultimately affecting your self-esteem.

How is your self-esteem affected? If you become anxious and withdraw and you have only the negative reactions of others to evaluate your own behavior, you might conclude that you are an unreliable and irresponsible person. Or, if you become aggressive, you might conclude that you are a hostile, fly-off-the-handle woman! Not knowing about the physical basis of PMS can hurt your self-esteem because you can put too much faith in a conventional image of how you are supposed to act, and you punish yourself mentally for your behavior.

From the Outside In

When you are premenstrual, factors outside yourself—a frown on someone's face, a cynical remark—can trigger off a series of physiological reactions that can result in sudden mood and behavioral changes. You may tend to overreact emotionally to what someone says or does. Within a short period of time, you can go from feeling OK to feeling awful.

If you are suffering from severe PMS, your perspective is probably affected and problems coming from the outside world can feel overwhelming. The state of your mind and body can prevent you from acting in your own behalf. In other words, severe PMS can leave you in a state of despair about the possibility of trying to gain control of the situation. This is a major problem associated with PMS.

What is to be Undone?

Frequently, women tell me that they deal with the same issue in different ways at different times of the month. Through charting, you can see if you do this yourself. You might find, for example, that during your good time, you and your husband might disagree about who is going to use the car on a particular day. But it is simply that: a little disagreement.

During your bad time, the same disagreement occurs. This time, however, there's a major blowup. You can therefore conclude that the problem this time is not who uses the car. The real problem is PMS.

A small issue, in other words, is likely to get blown out of proportion and intensified when you are premenstrual. Problems that are manageable during non-PMS times become unmanageable during PMS times.

Feeling Wronged

If you are like other women who suffer from PMS, your perceptions of reality might change when you are premenstrual. You can easily feel wronged, certain that your perceptions are correct and that the other person is simply unable to see what's really going on. Your sense of what is happening—as opposed to how others perceive the same events—can make you suspicious and critical. You may react with a blunt rebuke or a sarcastic remark.

Keep in mind that when you are premenstrual, your tolerance for other people's perceptions is probably strained. So if you are sarcastic or devastatingly critical—without any apparent tolerance of the other person's viewpoint—you will probably be dealt with similarly. The other person will react to you in kind, hurting your feelings. The other person will feel equally angry and upset.

What Are You Really Saying?

Your perceptions may be correct, but your tone and attitude may be inappropriate—at least as far as the other person is concerned. Remember that you communicate with your whole being, not just with words. The tone of your voice, the look on your face, and your body language convey your message. As Grace, 36, an astronomer, said:

> *After I've been in an argument, I go over my words again and again. I just know that what I was saying was right. It's not until later, when I reflect upon everything again, that I begin to realize that the other person is seeing and hearing the whole thing—not just what I'm saying, but also how I sound and the way I look.*

Keep in mind that the person with whom you are speaking receives all these cues.

Nobody Understands

If you are like other women who suffer from PMS, you probably deal with your bad times by withdrawing. More than one woman has said to me, "I want to be alone with my madness."

This tends to make the situation worse, not better. You withdraw and do not respond to your friends. After a while, they stop trying to get in touch with you. When they do not contact you, this convinces you that you are not worth their friendship. As Carolyn, 39, a divorced mother with one child said:

> *I've lost most of my friends. People don't understand. I cancel out and people don't understand.*

LET'S GET THINGS BACK IN PERSPECTIVE

Rather than spending energy asserting that your perceptions of the world are best, correct, and the only ones, you need to rechannel some of this energy. It will be of far greater value to you if you become more tuned into yourself and what is happening to you.

For the moment, take comfort in the fact that what you are experiencing—your thought processes and your behavior—are common for women who suffer from PMS. You are not to blame for this medical disorder. In the long run, it is crucial to see where these patterns of thought and behavior come from so that you can take action and turn things around.

Take a Positive Approach

Enlist the aid of those closest to you. The solution to your angry outbursts is not to withdraw, which alienates you from others. Ask your family and friends for their empathy, understanding and support. Try calling a friend to go for a walk. If you are by yourself, go to the YWCA where you can swim or run and not be completely alone. The idea is to be around other people, even though you don't have to interact directly with them.

CHAPTER 5

GETTING HELP:

Problems and Solutions

PATRICIA'S DIARY

Aug 1984	*Went for counseling. The counselor suggested I do something outside the house. Felt immobilized, didn't act on her suggestions.*
Nov 1984	*Realized I was screaming at the kids and felt like I was spanking them in anger.*
Apr 1985	*Went back for counseling because of problems at home—not getting along with Al and the kids. Became involved with Parents Anonymous because I was afraid I would hurt my children.*
Jun 1985	*Felt stressed out, had chronic sinus problems and headaches. Went for a physical. Doctor put me on antibiotics and muscle relaxants for stress and tight muscles. Didn't help, so he sent me to a nose specialist who suggested a sinus operation. I had an operation to help with the headaches. Recovered breathing better, but still had the headaches.*
Sep 1985	*Saw a show on PMS. I knew that I must be one of the women who have PMS 3 weeks out of the month. So I went back to the doctor with my information on PMS. Told him I had mood swings and depression before my period. He referred me to a psychiatrist. I was put on a waiting list.*
Dec 1985	*Started weekly visits in November. Even though I was in*

	counseling, there were still problems with our marriage. Separated from my husband.
Mar 1986	*Divorced. I still can't maintain a stable life. I have spent so much money trying to get help, and after spending $1,800 on sessions with the psychiatrist, he says I am not crazy. I wish someone could help me. Now that I'm divorced, I can't afford all these psychiatric appointments, but I can't survive on my own either.*
	I've lost my husband, and it seems I don't have any more friends. It is not the stress resulting from these things that causes my symptoms. It is the symptoms that cause my inability to cope with and handle life's pressures.
	I am a strong fighter, but with every passing month I feel weaker and weaker from within, and sometimes life seems too much to bear.

YOU ARE NOT ALONE

Like all of us who have suffered from PMS, you probably feel that your life—to one degree or another—has been disrupted. Do you often feel sad, alone, depressed, and even desperate? Do you end up feeling out of control? Are you embarrassed about your behavior? Do you worry that your behavior is negatively affecting your family relationships and your work situation? Do you find yourself binging on sweets and salty foods? Do you find that you are trying to cope with your problems by turning to alcohol?

You are not alone. These feelings and behaviors are common to women who suffer from PMS. You are not the only one who at times feels crazy and full of self-doubt. You are not the only one who has worried about what you are doing to your family.

Your problems and search for help might not be as severe and rocky as Patricia's story. But if you have been suffering from PMS for a while, chances are that you have sought help without much success. However, you have two advantages that Patricia did not have. The body of literature about PMS has expanded, and the medical community is becoming more aware of PMS.

Even so, there are several reasons why you may not receive correct information, appropriate diagnosis and proper treatment for PMS. In this chapter, we will discuss the following factors that may interfere with your search for help:

- PMS can debilitate you and make it difficult for you to seek professional help.
- Problems such as stereotyping and common myths can make you feel victimized by PMS.
- The medical profession's approach to PMS can lead to misdiagnosis and mistreatment of this disorder.

But keep in mind that PMS is manageable and can be treated. Because there are effective treatments for PMS, you need not feel victimized by it.

In the second half of this chapter we will discuss the best ways for you to obtain help and suggest several ways for you to start rebuilding your self-esteem.

FEELING CONFUSED AND VULNERABLE

How do you get help for PMS? Cautiously and sometimes with great difficulty. In order to ask for help, you must be clear about what you need. You must also be positive and assertive. But PMS can make you feel:

- Doubtful about how you really feel
- Confused
- Embarrassed
- Vulnerable
- Paranoid
- Depressed

Symptoms of PMS—such as confusion and depression—can be barriers in the search for help. This means that when you need help the most, it is particularly difficult to ask for it. You can feel so confused and depressed that making a telephone call to set up an appointment seems like an impossible or futile task. Moreover, when

Take a Positive Approach

No matter how many people have said that your symptoms are all in your head, there *is* something you can do to help yourself. You need to be very clear about this: You are no longer debilitated or incapacitated if you are acting on the problem. You are informing yourself and seeking help. Despite how vulnerable you feel, *you have already taken the first step*. You have started to regain control.

you make an appointment, you might eventually cancel it. Why? When you feel good again, you convince yourself that you do not really have a problem, so you withdraw your request for help.

When you are premenstrual, you are least clear about your symptoms and most vulnerable and easily confused. It is also the time when you are least able to discuss your symptoms in such a way that your doctor will listen attentively and take you seriously.

Getting help for PMS requires self-understanding, patience and persistence. In the self-help exercise below, think about how far you have come already. Recognize your own positive action and thank yourself for "helping you out"! In spite of the great odds against you, you have persevered. Recognize your own role. Congratulate yourself.

FEELING VICTIMIZED BY PMS

Now that you have become aware of problems that can develop in your own mind, such as feelings of confusion and vulnerability, you also need to become aware of problems that are created by the attitudes and beliefs of others. Not knowing about the relationship between physical and psychological changes can create confusion for

---

Self-Help Exercise

CONGRATULATIONS

Write a congratulations card for yourself. You deserve it. What might you write on this card?

- "Good for you! You have identified the problem."
- "Good for you! You have sought help."
- "Good for you! You have started to act. I bet you feel lighter and free of some of the extra baggage that you have been carrying around for a long time."
- "Good for you! You have persisted and persevered."
- "I appreciate what you have done for yourself and your family." Now you can begin to ______________________________

  ____

  ____

you and others, making it more difficult to get understanding and treatment. This kind of frustration was expressed by Jeri as:

> *I feel defeated every single month.*

If you (and others) do not understand how the physical changes in your body interact with your emotions and state of mind, you can understandably feel powerless. Lack of information and knowledge equates with not being able to resolve the problem. This feeling of powerlessness is a form of victimization.

Stereotypes

Stereotyping about PMS has its origins in both commonly held views and psychological theories. The problem is that commonly held views contain a lot of *myth-information*—myths and misinformation. You might be judging your behavior according to this myth-information. For example, many people believe that a woman's premenstrual symptoms indicate that she is going through an early menopause or is "going crazy."

Stereotyping about PMS has succeeded in portraying women negatively in many different ways, including the following:

- The woman has difficulty accepting her female role.
- She is repressing her sexuality.
- She has a negative attitude toward her body.
- She has a negative attitude toward menstruation.[19]

Unfortunately, these are not simply stereotypes. Often they are psychological theories, with names such as *gender identity crisis*. Fortunately, however, current medical research is now focusing more on the biochemical components of depression and similar kinds of disorders.[20]

I'm Not Being Taken Seriously

We can also feel victimized by PMS because it makes us feel that our thoughts and feelings are dismissed when we are premenstrual. Even when we act on our problems, the outcome can be frustrating. Rebecca, 37, married and the mother of three, explained it this way:

> *I feel victimized by PMS because my husband knows that I suffer from it, so he doesn't take me as seriously as before. Instead of being more understanding, now he just dismisses things that I say because he attributes them to my PMS.*

This woman is afraid of not being taken seriously. Other women express this kind of fear in stronger terms. They say they feel victimized because to say that they have PMS is equated with admitting that they are ruled by hormones . . . so-called "raging hormones." This can be quite upsetting. Beth, 35, an English professor at a major university, voiced this concern:

> *Before, if a man said something to me about raging hormones, I would have flown into a fit of justified anger. It seems so anti-feminist. Now, I'm supposed to say this myself?*

No, you are not supposed to say this! We are not in any way ruled by our hormones. But it is indeed a form of victimization not to know about the interaction of the way we feel and the way we think—the interaction of the body and the mind.

Let's Think About What's Really Going On

There are several issues to consider. Let's separate them out and look at each one individually.

- Saying that you suffer from a medical disorder is being equated with *admitting* something.
- You fear that if you acknowledge that you suffer from PMS, you are saying that you are not capable or responsible.
- Saying that you feel weak, vulnerable and out of control makes you think that you have to go along with commonly held—but erroneous—ideas about what it means to be a woman.

To be afraid to say that you are affected by PMS is definitely a legitimate issue. Why? Because you may be stereotyped by others and judged irresponsible. Their (mis)beliefs can prevent them from taking you seriously. This erodes your sense of self-knowledge and self-confidence, and jeopardizes your position and status.

Awareness of PMS Can Be A Double-Edged Sword

Increasing awareness of PMS in the lay and medical communities makes it easier for a woman who is suffering from the disorder to get help. However, superficial knowledge of PMS can fuel some people's false notions that women are victims of their own biological processes and cannot act rationally or responsibly.

These attitudes can understandably make women who suffer from PMS feel defeated, victimized and powerless because:

- Sometimes women cannot find out what is happening to them even when they take the initiative to do so.

- Women are sometimes given incorrect information and treatment from medical professionals.
- Women are still being viewed and judged by centuries of myths and misinformation.

Women today are pioneering social change because we are examining and questioning stereotypes about PMS. Significant social change comes only after a painful period of examination and confrontation. Myths and stereotypes die hard, but they do indeed fade away when challenged. We can be hopeful that things will be better for women of the future. We should not be afraid of knowledge about PMS, because knowledge shatters misinformation.

BE FOREWARNED

Patricia's story at the beginning of this chapter is a common one at the PMS Clinic. The medical profession has often prescribed addictive drugs and, in some cases, performed unnecessary operations in an attempt to treat PMS. It may sound ironic, but you should be wary when you decide to ask a doctor for help. If you don't, your problem might be misdiagnosed and mistreated. As Patricia's story suggests, there can be negative consequences for your body, your mind, your family life and your pocketbook. First we will discuss why so much confusion exists about PMS. Then we will discuss the consequences of this.

Take a Positive Approach

If you sense that others are criticizing and condemning your premenstrual behavior, it is up to you to take action so that you will not feel defeated and powerless. Inform those who are in a position to evaluate you that you are suffering from a medical disorder for which you are receiving treatment. You are not obligated to discuss the particulars of your personal health with those who employ you or others with whom you come into contact. Neither are you responsible for changing their stereotypical and misinformed thinking. However, you *are* responsible for your own well-being and whatever might affect it.

Skepticism About PMS

PMS was described over 50 years ago by Dr. Robert T. Frank of New York. In 1931, he wrote the first article about PMS entitled, "The Hormonal Causes of Premenstrual Tension." PMS was first treated successfully over 30 years ago in Great Britain. Today premenstrual syndrome is receiving attention in professional medical journals. However, my experience with doctors suggests that some are unfamiliar with current articles and research about PMS.

As a result, information in the press or information that a woman provides a doctor tends to be received skeptically. That is, if a doctor's only knowledge of PMS is acquired via the news media, and the news media sensationalize the subject, then the doctor may perceive PMS to be the latest fad. As a result, the doctor may be skeptical of what the patient is saying. The patient may be fairly certain that she has PMS, but the doctor thinks she has merely been influenced by what she has read or seen on TV.

Ironically, despite doctors' skepticism about PMS, they frequently (mis)treat PMS with tranquilizers. They try to relieve the psychological symptoms of PMS, overlooking the fact that it is physical in origin.

Lack of a Holistic Approach to PMS

When you talk to your doctor about your cyclical anxiety, irritability, depression and headaches, he or she may not think to look for a physical cause. The specialization of knowledge within the medical profession results in many doctors having limited knowledge of the physical bases of psychological problems.

If a doctor is unaware of a woman's typical pattern of hormonal fluctuation, he or she is unlikely to see the relationship between a change in your mental state and where you are in your menstrual cycle. As a result, your depressed or anxious state of mind may be viewed as an isolated phenomenon, unrelated to the cycles of your body.

Significant hormonal fluctuation takes place at different points in your life: puberty, pregnancy, postpartum and menopause. Significant hormonal fluctuation also occurs within your body each month. If both you and your doctor are unaware of the cyclical nature of PMS, confusion will reign supreme! There may be little or no ability to explain why you feel terrible during one visit to your doctor and fine the next, or vice versa, despite the fact that you are taking your medication as prescribed. Or, your doctor might diagnose your symptoms—a seizure or a migraine, for example—as random events totally unrelated to your menstrual cycle.

Ups and Downs with the Therapist

A very confusing situation also can arise if you begin seeing a therapist regularly and neither you nor your therapist knows about PMS. For instance, you may feel depressed during the first couple of visits. A few days after seeing the therapist, you might begin to feel better and decide that therapy is the key to eliminating your anxiety and depression. You may receive confirmation of this the next time you see your therapist—you do indeed feel very good and your therapist congratulates you on your progress.

The next visit, however, you may be in a terrible mood. Neither you nor your therapist can understand why, after having made significant progress, you are now feeling so down again.

Your therapist may think, "I don't understand what's going on here. I saw her 2 weeks ago, and she felt so good about herself, her family, and everything in her life. Now, she's right back where she started."

The odds are about 50-50 that the first time you visit your doctor or therapist you will seem fine. But the next time, for no apparent reason, you will not. Without charting, neither you or your doctor or therapist will be able to explain the changes in your physical and psychological state.

I often recommend to people in the helping professions that they encourage every female client to chart her symptoms to discover if her anxiety and depression are linked with her menstrual cycle. From my perspective, this seems essential.

If you're working with a therapist, it's very important that you inform him or her that you're investigating the possibility that you might have PMS. If he or she doesn't seem well-informed about PMS, take the initiative to suggest some reading in this area. References on pages 168-169 can be helpful.

You Are Not a Hypochondriac

Not surprisingly, many women who suffer from PMS think that they are hypochondriacs. Reassurance from your doctor that you are fine may add to your fear of being called a hypochondriac, because such reassurance can make you think you are imagining that you do not feel well. You might even wish that your doctor could find something wrong with you to explain why you feel so badly.

You will feel less like a hypochondriac and less crazy when you realize, first, that you are not alone. You are in territory familiar to many women. Second, there are many reasons why you might feel like a hypochondriac that have *nothing to do with you*. You may have been badly advised in a number of different ways.

Your doctor might be telling you that there is nothing wrong with you, but your body is saying something quite different! Moreover, you may feel that the doctor's advice—given in good faith—is turned around and used as ammunition against you. Your family or friends might say, "But the doctor says that there is nothing wrong with you!"

Myth-Information

If You Are Told . . .	It Can Mean . . .
This is part of being a woman, my dear.	*What you experience is nothing out of the ordinary. You do not have a medical problem.*
You should seek counseling.	*There is nothing physically wrong with you. It is all in your head.*
There is nothing that can be done about it.	*You should learn to live with it. The medical and mental-health professions cannot help you.*

No wonder you feel like a hypochondriac. If your doctor suggests that there is nothing physically wrong with you, he or she may then advise you to see a therapist. This will reinforce the idea to you that the problem is all in your head. If you felt a little crazy before, you will probably feel really crazy now! More than once, a woman has told me:

> *I really am crazy. They all told me that I was fine, but I've got aches and pains, and sometimes I think that I'm dying because I feel so lousy.*

If you do not get confirmation from your doctor that your problems are real, you may conclude that you are suffering from an unknown disease. Because you sense something is wrong, and because you believe that the medical community should be able to explain the problem (but they fail to), you may harbor secret thoughts that you have an unknown disease that has yet to be discovered. Many women reach this conclusion and even feel that they may die before the cause of the problem is discovered.

Despite what everyone is saying, *you* know something is wrong because you *feel* your aches, pains, anger and depression. You probably have an intuitive feeling that it is related in some way to your menstrual cycle. In fact, when you first become informed about PMS, you might say what many other women have said to me:

I just knew it had something to do with my cycle and my hormones.

You need to start self-help measures as soon as you can to treat the problem. You might also consider getting some counseling to help rebuild your self-esteem and repair relationships that may have suffered.

HELPING YOURSELF

I encourage you to learn as much as you can about your body and trust your own judgment about how you feel. Trust that you are beginning to take responsibility for your own problems. For a starter, this means not putting your sense of self—your knowledge about what is happening to you, your self-confidence, and your self-esteem—into the hands of others.

You Are in Charge

Because you know yourself better than anyone else, your self-observation is invaluable in treating PMS. However, I am not suggesting that you be your own doctor. You need to be open-minded and listen to expert advice. A team approach to PMS can be very effective, especially if your symptoms are not relieved significantly with self-help measures. PMS can feel overwhelming and you might understandably need assistance.

Do not pass up an opportunity to get good information that might help relieve your symptoms. Perhaps medical advice from a well-informed physician would be helpful, or you might need counseling from a professional who understands the dynamics of PMS. A team approach is a good idea because then you don't have to solve the problem by yourself. Listen carefully and take advantage of the expertise of others. Trust yourself, and trust that with the help of supportive professionals you can arrive at a satisfactory solution.

Characteristics of a Good Clinic

You might choose to go to a PMS clinic. If so, check for certain characteristics when you are looking for a clinic. Because PMS is such a multifaceted syndrome, it involves more than medical issues. Look for a clinic that provides emotional, psychological and medical support. The following services should be included and affordable:

- One-to-one counseling
- Group sessions
- Couple counseling
- Information seminars

- Ongoing support groups
- Medical supervision
- Referral services (for alcoholism, eating problems, etc.)

When You Seek Help

Go for assistance when you feel most capable, most confident and most self-assured. Go when you feel best able to communicate clearly. Take advantage of the good time of your cycle to communicate your concerns and needs. Be as informed as possible about your mental and physical condition when talking to your doctor and your counselor. Then listen carefully to what they have to say.

If you have charted your symptoms, it is an excellent idea to take these charts with you when you seek help for PMS. Your charts document for your doctor or therapist exactly what has been happening with you. This eliminates any guessing games about your symptoms. What you have documented are facts, and facts cannot be denied. Your charts are evidence that you regularly act and feel differently at different times of the month.

Keep These Points in Mind

- You have taken the initiative to get professional assistance. Give yourself credit.
- The symptoms of PMS are debilitating and can strip away your self-confidence. Don't add to your problems by using other people's labels and stereotypes to condemn yourself.
- PMS has been amply documented in mainstream professional medical journals. If necessary, bring these to the attention of your doctor or therapist.
- Your therapist may not be well-versed about PMS, but you have a right to expect him or her to willingly explore all avenues with you. If your therapist is not receptive to this, your time may be better spent looking for a different counselor.
- Approach the issue of PMS in such a way that it will not be used against you. If you need to discuss your health concerns with someone other than family or close friends, you can say that you are having problems with a medical disorder (without naming PMS). Be sure to let them know that, with treatment, you expect to get it under control within a reasonable amount of time.

One final word about getting help. Other women have been successful in getting PMS under control. You can too. As Holly told me:

> *After living 16 years in a nightmare, trying to figure out why my life was such a roller-coaster ride, I now feel like I'm in a dream world. My*

children and I finally get along, and I like myself for the first time in a long time. Going to the PMS Clinic was one of the most positive things I've done for myself.

REBUILDING YOUR PSYCHOLOGICAL FOUNDATION

Exploring and discovering how self-esteem is gained and lost is very valuable. As you come to understand the physical and psychological symptoms associated with PMS, it will help you gain a sense of how you can change your thought patterns and behavior. You will want to know how to rebuild your self-esteem, learn again to evaluate yourself fairly, and regain a positive self-image.

Rediscover Yourself

Self-esteem is derived from a sense of personal worth. A healthy sense of self means that you trust your own intuitions and rely on your personal judgment. These are not characteristics that you (or anyone else) inherits at birth. Rather, these are learned behavioral traits. How can you develop these?

You will be happier and more generous with yourself and others if you know your specific strengths and admirable characteristics. Make a list of these, and keep it handy to bring out whenever you feel your self-esteem ebbing. This is learning to like yourself so that you can be loving and gentle toward yourself and others.

Self-Help Exercise

HOW DO YOU DO?

1. Introduce your "self" to you. Act this out. Act the same way that you would if you were introducing or being introduced at a party—compliment yourself, ask about your friends, family, etc.
2. What do you notice about yourself that you like and admire? Is it the tone of your voice? Is it your smile? Is it what you say?
3. What do you perceive about yourself that is self-defeating? Are you too critical? Are you too quick to jump to conclusions?
4. Now demonstrate to yourself that you have traits that other people admire. Introduce yourself to someone else, mentioning these admirable charactertistics to them.

Set Realistic Goals

Self-esteem is derived from a sense of personal effectiveness. You gain a sense of personal effectiveness from setting realistic goals that you can accomplish. When you decide what is feasible—and do it—you feel a sense of accomplishment. When you mentally note what you have accomplished and give yourself credit for doing it, you begin to feel your effectiveness. For example, if you decide you need to exercise because you have not exercised for a year, a realistic goal is to begin by taking a short walk. If you walk a little every day, you soon feel that you are accomplishing your goal. You start to feel personally effective.

However, if you decide that you must start running 5 miles every day, you will probably run once or twice and give up. In addition to not getting any exercise, you will disappoint yourself, feel guilty about not running, and mentally chastise yourself. Setting high expectations that are not realistic leads quickly to anger and disappointment with yourself. You feel ineffective, and your self-esteem suffers. Setting realistic goals that you carry out makes you feel that you are effective and can achieve what you set out to do.

Distinguish Your "Real Self" and Your "PMS Self"

As a woman with PMS, you can improve your sense of personal worth by distinguishing between your "real self" and your "PMS self." You can begin to separate and think about your different behaviors. Then, when you are premenstrual and do something that makes you feel anxious and guilty, you can properly categorize it as PMS behavior. This helps you be less harsh in judging yourself. This does not excuse the behavior, but it helps you put it in perspective. In this way, you do not tear down the self-esteem that you have just started to rebuild.

If you have a tendency to be harsh with yourself and think it necessary always to appear in control of things, you most likely will criticize your behavior when something goes wrong. In fact, none of it should be harshly judged, some should be modified, and the rest praised. In the self-help exercise on the opposite page, look at the sample comparisons of how you might feel when you are premenstrual and when you are not premenstrual. Fill in the blanks with your own sentiments.

Listen to Your Mental Chatter

Your private logic is constantly reinforced—either built up or torn down—by what you say to yourself and how you say it. Your mental patterns begin to develop in childhood. They change as you go through life's experiences and typically proceed without your being aware of them. It is important to become aware of your mental habits and pay attention to how you "talk to yourself."

The way you talk to yourself can be as helpful, sympathetic and supportive as your best friend talking to you. On the other hand, it can be as panic-provoking as when your boss criticizes you. Your mental chatter can see you through a crisis and let you

Self-Help Exercise

VIVE LA DIFFERENCE!

The Me I Like	The Premenstrual Me
I can be trusted.	*I am catty and backbiting.*
I like getting involved and making a commitment.	*I start something, but then it fizzles.*
I like people.	*I hate myself, and everyone irritates me.*
I enjoy listening to others.	*When other people talk, it annoys me.*
I value my ability to learn and my concern for people.	*Everything I do or say is messed up.*
I feel healthy.	*I feel horrible.*
I feel like I have a purpose in life.	*I feel worthless and purposeless.*
I know of people who love me and really care about me.	*My partner and kids would be better off without me.*
____________________	____________________
____________________	____________________
____________________	____________________
____________________	____________________
____________________	____________________
____________________	____________________
____________________	____________________
____________________	____________________

float above the storm. Or, it can be catastrophic, creating a sense of anxiety that impedes you from achieving what you set out to do. Just as you seek out some people and avoid others, you can begin to note and reinforce the positive statements that you make to yourself—and avoid making negative statements. Once you become aware of the things that you say to yourself, you can begin to sort through these statements. Eliminate those that are detrimental to your self-esteem, and reinforce those that help you be supportive of your own efforts. The exercise opposite can help you.

Develop Some Strategies

Some women with PMS have developed techniques to stay calm during moments of crisis. If you have PMS, it is very important that you develop a technique that will work for you. You should plan your strategy in advance because when you are in a moment of crisis, you might not be able to think clearly or have the desire to devise a strategy. Here are some useful strategies that I encourage you to use.

- Look at the calendar. Are you premenstrual?
- Go to another room and close the door. Put on some calming music, take a hot bath, read a book, or write down how you are feeling.
- Do something physically active. Take a walk or go for a run. Get away from an all-or-nothing approach, such as, "Either I run 5 miles or I do nothing."

One young girl suffered from PMS to such an extent that she was hospitalized for 3 months after several suicide attempts. Once her problem was diagnosed and treated, she told me of her very pragmatic strategy:

> *I tell myself over and over, "It's PMS, it's PMS." I even ask my friends to tell me this. And they do—because I forget, but they don't. Then I figure that whatever is bothering me could either be caused by PMS or not. If it is PMS, it will disappear after a while. If it's not, then the problem will still be there later when I am able to deal with it.*

Develop a Positive Addiction

What do you regularly do for yourself? What do you do on a daily basis that you like and make no excuses to yourself about doing?

- Exercise?
- Read?
- Play music?
- Write?

The next time you feel yourself going into a premenstrual slump, use your own positive addiction immediately!

Self-Help Exercise

CHATTING WITH YOURSELF

1. Become aware of your own mental chatter. Over the next few days, note the typical kinds of statements that you make to yourself and jot these down.
2. Evaluate your mental chatter. Are you friendly toward yourself? Do you compliment yourself? Do you criticize yourself? Do you hurry yourself? Do you make yourself feel guilty?
3. Write down the statements that you make to yourself that help you most.

    ____

    ____

    ____

    ____

In other words, encourage yourself to develop good habits—mental and physical—so that you can call on them during a time of crisis.

Pat Yourself on the Back

Your sense of self-worth is influenced by external sources, but ultimately it rests on the internal satisfaction you derive from your own efforts and accomplishments. The ability to regain some control over your life and acknowledge your own positive role in this process will contribute to a renewed sense of worth. You will derive satisfaction from meeting realistic expectations. An increase in self-esteem will be confirmed when you tell yourself, "I'm doing the best I can." When you acknowledge your active role in this process, you are beginning to rebuild your sense of personal worth.

As you grow in self-acceptance and begin to believe in your own personal feelings and intuition again, you will be less harsh with yourself and more trusting of your personal feelings. The people around you will come to respect you for your faith in yourself. You will move away from an all-or-nothing approach to life and begin to gain satisfaction for achieving the little things (and big things) that you set out to do. You will not fear making a mistake. You will develop the courage to be imperfect, to live with your humanity and not be upset by the realities of mistakes. Mistakes will become opportunities to learn and grow. You will be able to look back and maybe even laugh at your behavior. Certainly you will learn from it.

CHAPTER 6

Family Dynamics:

PMS and Your Family

TERESA'S STORY

I really am a good mom. But during those days, I don't know how my kids can stand to be around me . . .

Sometimes, I can do it all. I make sure that all the things they need for school are ready on time. I also drive the car pool, and I'm a room mother at school. I make sure that they get to their lessons, and I pick them up from practice. I make sure that their diets are well-balanced. I'm even a friend to their friends. You might say I'm everybody's favorite mother—during my good times.

But then I turn into an ogre, and it makes their heads spin. I can see the destruction I cause right in front of me. Here's what I mean. I get a phone call from my little boy, for instance, asking me to come and pick him up at practice 15 minutes early. Depending on the time of the month, I either say, "Oh, good, you get to come home early," or I screech, "What? Do you think I'm a taxi service?"

My husband can become alarmed at my behavior and step in. If I'm screaming, he tells me to calm down. If the kids need to be taken somewhere, he takes them. He takes the kids to the backyard or another room—anywhere else—to remove them. He's like a buffer zone. He says to the kids, "She'll be OK. She's just upset now. Let's go outside and play for a while." He creates diversions.

My reactions to my husband are mixed. In the past, I resented it if he stepped in. Usually I didn't talk with him about it until after some time had gone by. And then I would confront him with, "You're treating me like I'm an incompetent mother."

Now I realize that he really does think I'm a good mother. If he steps in, it's probably necessary. When I have doubts, the looks on my kids' faces are enough to tell me that I really am acting crazy. So now I'm more grateful and relieved, but I also feel less in control of the situation.

I feel like my husband has helped me identify a real problem. Now he calls me during the day to see how I'm doing. I like his support, but it also tends to confirm my worst fears that I'm not a good mother. Sometimes I think, "They'd be better off without me."

WHO IS TAKING CARE OF WHOM?

Healthy family dynamics mean that family members give and receive emotional support. However, PMS can shake the emotional-psychological foundation of the family. The following statement from Denise suggests just how unstable the family situation can become as a result of PMS:

> *During that time of the month, my family has to be on guard because I take it out on the ones I love the most. I reserve my nastiness for my family.*

PMS issues involve the whole family. With PMS, emotional confusion and turmoil can build up for everyone involved. You might sense that family relationships are disintegrating and that your family is suffering as much as you are.

Women often take responsibility for emotions of the family. We tend to be caretakers. We often take care of our families before we take care of ourselves. If you have PMS, think about how ironic this is: you are trying to take responsibility for your family's emotional needs at the very time when you feel out of control.

In this chapter we are going to discuss how your emotions and psychological state of mind can directly affect your family. We will discuss how your family can become confused and upset. We will also discuss how different family members react to your PMS and how you can best talk with them about your situation. Finally, we are going to talk about how gaining your family's support is a crucial element in getting better.

TRYING TO BE CONSISTENT

Parents are often advised to be consistent with their children. When you are suffering from PMS, you know that the last thing you are is consistent. This can be a genuine dilemma. As Suzanne, a mother of three children, expressed worriedly:

> *How can I be consistent? One minute I feel OK, and the next I feel like I'm going nuts.*

Keep in mind that, by its nature, PMS may make you feel moody, confused and inconsistent. When you are premenstrual, the problem can be that what you want and what you expect are two different things. Often women express this kind of ambivalence in ways that sound contradictory, such as:

> *I want space, but I don't want to be left alone.*
>
> *I need tons of love, but I don't let anyone give it to me.*

Because of your conflicting needs, you probably send mixed messages. Not surprisingly, this confuses your family. They might not know what to expect, and they don't necessarily know how to help you. It may seem to them that half the time they can believe what you are saying and half the time they can't. This can pose a dilemma for them. For self-protection, they will probably develop feelings of ambivalence and act ambivalently toward you.

Self-Help Exercise

WHO NEEDS WHAT?

1. List your needs—especially emotional needs—when you are premenstrual.
   ____
   ____

2. To what extent do your needs contradict each other? ______________
   ____

3. What arrangements can you make with your family when you must take care of yourself?
   ____
   ____
   ____

AM I LEAVING SCARS?

Every mother wants her children to be well-adjusted and to like her. However, you can feel most distant from your children at the time when you are premenstrual.

When I was suffering from PMS, my son once told me, "You're just like Cinderella's stepmother—mean and ugly."

The worst part was that I knew he was right. I got that sick feeling in the pit of my stomach, and I thought to myself:

> *I've done it again. I've got to stop doing this. I'm hurting my children.*

But what did I do? Like other women whom I counsel, I withdrew. I thought that the best thing to do was to spare my family—spare them from me. Most women who come to the clinic share this feeling. They say to me:

> *I'm worried about what I'm doing to my kids.*

This worry can develop because you believe your premenstrual behavior is alienating your children and setting a negative example for how to cope with life's stresses. You are probably projecting onto them a lot of your own feelings. You feel alienated, so you assume that they do too. Many women say to me:

> *I may not be physically hurting my children, but I feel that I'm verbally abusing them.*

What you say to your children affects them, of course. It can make them feel guilty if you say things like, "You're driving me crazy," and then later say, "I feel like I'm going crazy. I can't stand this any more." Understandably, they may blame themselves for "making you go crazy."

Even if you are not doing or saying anything to hurt your children, you can create a lot of anxiety and tension when you are premenstrual that spills over into family relations. Linda, a mother of two school-age children, expressed her anxiety in the following way:

> *I dread the thought of the school break alone with the kids. I fear myself and what I could do in my anger.*

More often than not, what is actually bothering you is fear and anxiety that you *might* hurt your children. However, some women report losing their tempers and slapping their children. If this is the case with you, you are probably quite aware of what is happening, but feel unable to control it. As Mary, who has a 3-year-old daughter, told me:

> *I'd rather die than do something to harm my child, but sometimes I am so out of control that I lose my temper and smack her across the face.*

If you become angry and feel out of control, you probably feel separated from yourself and see yourself as acting out of character. This can increase your frustration and guilt. It is imperative that you not give in to an impulse to slap or in any way physically harm your children. You can always *remove yourself* from the situation, call an emergency number, or ask a friend or family member to help you.

THE SUPERMOM SYNDROME

If you are a mother, one of your greatest fears at times is that you are not a good mother. Other people are not saying this to you, but *you* may be telling yourself this. Why? Because your anxiety and guilt about premenstrual behavior builds up and carries over into your good time. Most likely you will try to overcompensate for your premenstrual behavior. As Judy said to me:

> *I try to be a supermom during my good time because I do so many bad things during my PMS time.*

Because you think that you acted badly when you were premenstrual, you think that you have to make up for your behavior when you feel back to normal again. The following scenario is an example of how many women overcompensate for their premenstrual behavior.

Because you feel guilty for being so short-tempered with the kids when you were premenstrual, it is not enough just to take the kids out for lunch. You decide to take them out to lunch *and* a movie. You know beforehand that the kids really need to be home by 5:30 for dinner, and you have to be at a dinner party by 6:30. But showing your kids that you love them has priority at the moment.

Almost predictably, you do not get back from the movie until 5:35. Everyone is stressed and angry. The kids are upset, and you have less than an hour to fix dinner for the children and get ready for the party. In the process of trying to do all this, you blow up at your husband, who is also running late because he got stuck in a traffic jam. Then you withdraw, get depressed, and refuse to go to the party.

The Vicious Cycle Repeated

The vicious cycle that is being played out here looks like this:

1. When you are premenstrual, you have trouble setting limits that you and the children can keep.
2. As a result, you become angry and blow up at them.

3. When you are feeling better again, you think that you have to make up to them.
4. However, you go overboard and try to do too much.
5. As a result, neither you or the children are happy.
6. As a spinoff, you become angry with your partner.
7. You withdraw and think that your family would be better off without you.
8. You also entertain the idea that you would be better off without them.
9. Your behavior leaves you and your family feeling anxious and guilty.

Overcompensating for your premenstrual behavior clearly causes more, not fewer, problems.

Displacing Responsibility

Usually those who are closest to us are the targets for our anger and resentment. We blame them for our own problems. Subsequently we try to convince them—by overcompensating—that they really aren't the cause of our problems. All this does, however, is cause confusion and resentment.

The problem with overcompensating is that we are not actually taking care of our family. What we are doing is making them feel anxious and guilty for our actions. Often we are displacing onto them the responsibility for our actions because we are having difficulty facing our own problems. If you want to show your family that you love them, don't ask them to take responsibility for your actions.

REVERSING ROLES

Typically, when you are premenstrual, you may not be acting as alert, decisive, or responsibly as you normally would. People around you may develop a tendency—often unconsciously—to carry out your responsibilities. You might become forgetful and confused, for example, so your partner starts to take over in the kitchen. Your children might begin worrying about you.

What is happening is that your spouse and children are reversing roles with you. They feel that they are responsible for your situation (probably because you have often declared this). They are beginning to believe that something is wrong with *them*.

Take a Positive Approach

Think of your premenstrual behavior as history. The only way to make up for your premenstrual behavior is to not repeat it. The best way to do this is to take care of yourself. Family relationships will then heal.

Kids Also Overcompensate

Your irritability, anxiety and anger can lead your children to wonder: "What did I do to make Mom so angry?"

Children can easily assume that they are the cause of your anger. If so, they are acting in the same way as children whose parents are going through a divorce. They are blaming themselves for causing problems for which they are not responsible. When they feel guilty and overcompensate, they are taking responsibility for issues and problems that are not their own. Because they are trying to meet your needs, they are probably not meeting their own.

If you look at the situation from their perspective, you can see that they have good reason to blame themselves. Generally speaking, their environment is not stable or predictable. This is because you are not responding to situations in a consistent fashion. They may have done something last week, for example, that did not make you angry. This week, however, the same event did make you angry. Your children don't know when they are OK and when they are not. This is very frustrating for them. Because they are not in control of the situation, they blame themselves. As a result, some children become overcommitted and try even harder to make everything better. What is happening is that they are trying to be more in control of themselves when actually it is the family that is out of balance.

Dad's Role Can Change Too

When a woman suffers from PMS, it often affects the father's role. As a result, sometimes the father's role is clearly defined and sometimes it is not.

During part of the month, your partner will probably totally trust you "to be Mom." At other times of the month, he might send messages that say, "You're not capable of being Mom now. Let me take over."

This can seem to confirm your worst fears: "I'm crazy and incapable of raising my own children."

Keep in mind that the children's father is attempting to deal with the reality of the situation. You are not well, and he may feel that it is necessary to protect you and the children.

If you cannot control your temper and you are verbally or physically abusing your children, the children's father is likely to be very concerned. Women are quite aware of this. When I was counseling a couple, the woman said:

> *I felt like physically attacking my daughter. I felt like I was losing control.*

She looked at her husband very closely when she said this. Then she asked:

> *You do understand that I was feeling out of control, right?*

It was very important for her to get the message across to him that she was, indeed, losing control. She was looking for a reason for her feelings and kept checking with him, making eye contact with him, to find out if he believed her. It was as if she were saying, "See, I'm not crazy. I'm really not crazy."

Actually, he was not doubting her, nor was he skeptical of the idea that she was suffering from PMS. He clearly believed her. *She* was the one who was skeptical. Because she had lost confidence in herself, she assumed that her husband had too. Actually, he had just assumed a more protective role.

Not all men are sympathetic toward PMS, however, especially when it means that they have to take on extra responsibility. Instead of offering to help out, they might withdraw or try to become invisible! In a situation like this, it is important for you to draw on other people, such as good friends or relatives, for assistance.

A BACKDOOR APPROACH TO GETTING HELP

If you are like other women who seek help for PMS, you typically go to a clinic because you are worried about what you are doing to your family. You probably validate getting help for yourself by saying, as Valerie said to me:

> *If I can take care of this problem, then I can be a better mother for my children.*

If you justify getting counseling because it is for the sake of the family, this is a "backdoor approach" to taking care of yourself. Effectively, what you are saying is:

> *Who cares if I feel lousy? The important thing for me to do is take care of my family.*

Again, you are not alone. Many women come to the PMS Clinic for this reason. This approach comes from the attitude many women have that they should not spend money on themselves. It is not unusual for a woman to put her family's needs before her own. If you have PMS, it is even more likely. Why? Because PMS significantly contributes to low self-esteem. The last thing you are likely to do is spend time, money or energy on yourself. You may feel that you are not worth it, but you can justify getting help for the sake of your family. As I tell women who come to the PMS Clinic, "If this is what works for you, if this is the way you legitimize taking care of yourself, then use it for the time being."

THE RECOVERY PROCESS

We feel responsible for having torn apart relationships that are very important to us.

How do we go about putting the pieces back together and making our relationships stable again?

Keep in mind that you probably already feel quite alienated, and it does not make sense to alienate yourself even more by withdrawing "to be alone with your madness." As more than one woman has said to me:

> *I tell my family that I feel lousy. But when they ask what they can to to make it better, I usually say something like, "If I knew, don't you think I'd tell you?" Afterward I feel so guilty—they were just trying to help me.*

If you take this approach, what you are doing is getting angry with someone else for not being able to read your mind or figure out what you need. This is not fair to others, and it does not help you. Everyone feels guilty and ineffective, and no one wants to join forces to solve the problem.

You need to be aware of how deeply PMS can affect those with whom you live and interact. You are going to have to re-establish trust with your family. They are probably feeling a little shaky. You might not even trust yourself.

If you saw yourself as actively involved in destroying the family before, you can now see yourself as actively involved in helping your family. This is very important. It means there is hope for you and your family. As you get better, your family will go through a recovery process too. The following checkpoints are major ways in which you can begin the recovery process.

✔ *Ask for Help and Understanding*

When one family member is down, it is a good idea for the others to rally. Let your family help you. Although the temptation is to withdraw, it is not a good idea to shut out your family. Ask for help and understanding. You need to tell people in your family that they can be part of the solution and not just part of the problem. This way, you won't feel like you are destroying relationships, and you can start rebuilding your support system.

✔ *Approach PMS as a Physical Disorder*

It is imperative that families treat PMS as a physical disorder because this approach prevents guilt and resentment from building up. If family members do not, they might think: "Why are her problems so important? What am I supposed to do with my needs while we are taking care of her problems?"

During the time that this medical disorder is being treated, your family needs to make a concerted effort. As with any medical disorder, your family can help tremendously by becoming educated and acting on it. When PMS is treated as any other medical disorder, it is more likely to elicit compassion and understanding.

✔ *Take Responsibility for Yourself*

By being clear about what you need, you take your family out of the position of feeling responsible for your problems. Then they are in a better position to help you. Remember:

- Your family is not responsible for your problems.
- It is not a good idea if others feel guilty because you are not well.
- The family is not to blame for your actions.
- Family members are not inadequate if they can't read your mind and figure out the nature of your problem.

You are not to blame if you have PMS, just as you would not be to blame if you had diabetes. You are, however, responsible for your own well-being.

COMMUNICATION IS THE KEY

Much of what occurs within the family occurs at the psychological level. What is unspoken is as important as what is spoken. The more family members can express what is on their minds, the better.

We need to communicate with the people we love. We need to convey to them that we love them very deeply. It is important to be clear about the fact that PMS affects the way we act toward them. We need to do this so we are not left with the kind of guilt discussed earlier: "What have I done to my children?" The key is for us to be able to say what we want or expect from other family members. Use the following checkpoints in learning to communicate clearly:

✔ *Express How You Feel*

Describe your feelings so you can convey what it feels like to have PMS. You might tell your family that sometimes you feel like a prisoner in your own body, that you dislike what you do to yourself and others, and that you become frustrated and desperate as you watch yourself continue in such a negative vein. Remember that your family would prefer to empathize with you rather than be criticized by you.

✔ *Say Exactly What You Need*

It is a good idea for you to express exactly what you need (no matter how selfish it may sound). For example, you might say to your partner and children:

> *To take care of my emotional needs right now, I need extra space and extra understanding. What this means is that I would like to be alone in my room, but I would like you to stay around the house.*

Acknowledge the fact that these two things—wanting to be alone, but not wanting them to leave—do not go well together. It is an acknowledgment on our part of a dilemma that affects us and the whole family.

When you state exactly what you need, usually there will be a collective sigh of relief from your family. Now they don't have to feel responsible for guessing what you need. You can feel good because you have spoken clearly and have received from them a positive response. This opens the door for further communication.

✔ *Turn a Bad Situation into a Good One*

PMS can provide an opportunity for you to set a good example for your children. If you have been to several doctors without getting good results, you can talk with your children about the importance of persevering until you get the help you need. This shows them how to deal with adversity in a positive way. It is important to teach them to trust their instincts about their bodies.

✔ *Talk to Your Partner*

If you are really depressed and withdrawn, let your partner know that you might not be able to act. Be as clear as possible. Let him know that you need him to tune in. You might say:

> *This is the time that you need to take the initiative, especially with the kids.*

✔ *Talk to Your Kids*

It is very important for us to be able to reassure our children they are not the source of our problems. Although they might be young, do not underestimate their ability to understand.

Ideally, talk with each child one-on-one. What he or she needs to hear is something like this:

> *I want to talk with you about something that has to do with me. I want to tell you about it because you're important to me.*

State what you need as clearly as possible. Tell your child that you are dealing with a physical problem, and explain how this might affect him or her. You might say:

> *I'm dealing with PMS, which is a medical problem that affects my body and my attitude too. Sometimes it makes me feel bad all over. During those times, I'm not sure I know what is going to make me feel best. So I know it's tough for you to know as well.*

Or, if you are uncomfortable using the term PMS, tell your children that you are dealing with a hormonal imbalance in your body, without specifically naming it.

Although it sounds dramatic, it is important to let your kids know that you are not dying. Especially if they are young, they need to be reassured that you are going to be OK. If not, their imaginations can run wild, and they can easily conclude the worst. You might say:

> *I'm going to be OK. I'm getting help now. Of course, I am not going to die!*

By voicing what may be their deepest fear, you can remove the need for them to worry about you. This allows them to concentrate on helping with the problem.

Acknowledging the problem indicates to your children that you care about their feelings. It will also give them some insight about how they might best be able to interact with you. During the course of getting better, you might also say:

> *There may be times when I will ask you for extra help because I'm having a difficult day.*

Be sure to ask them for their opinions and their suggestions. Ask them what they think. By discussing how you feel and how it might affect them, you are giving them a sense of participation and a sense of being included in the solution to the problem. This is very important because it can help them feel more in control. Keep in mind that they have a control issue with PMS too.

After you tell them you have a physical problem, some children will immediately become involved in the conversation, ask questions, and pursue the topic. Others might not say anything. They might just sit there and seem not to react. But eventually—even if it is a week later—they will indicate that they have understood. They will probably bring up the subject of PMS on their own by asking a question about it. Take advantage of their curiosity to start a conversation. They are indicating that they like feeling included. It's a very positive indicator for both of you.

My suggestions for ways to talk with your children are, of necessity, general. Each child is different, and only you can select the words most appropriate for talking with your child. However you choose to approach the discussion, be confident that you are doing the right thing. Your behavior may have been bewildering to your children, and you are demystifying it for them. Known problems are much easier to cope with than unknowns. Talking to your children shows them that you respect them enough to trust them with the truth.

By being open, communicating and persevering, you are setting an excellent example for your children. You are showing them how to act responsibly when taking care of themselves. You are also showing them that part of the solution is in approaching the problem directly and positively.

Throughout this whole process, you are also legitimizing your own feelings and thoughts. You are hearing yourself say: "This is a medical problem." You are confirming your situation at the same time that you are building a support system for yourself. This is a very healthy approach to PMS.

PMS RUNS IN FAMILIES

Most of the evidence suggests that PMS runs in families. If you have PMS, most likely your mother did too. If your mother (or sister or grandmother) was often angry and teary, but also had times when everything seemed fine, she probably had PMS. Many women confirm that their mothers or sisters also had or have PMS. For example, 32-year-old Katherine, a high-school teacher, said:

> *I know my mother had it. She must have had it because her mood would swing all over the place, and I would never know what kind of mood she would be in. She was very unpredictable.*

As Katherine's recollection suggests, usually a woman's memories are of moodiness and a lot of unpredictability. By carrying out the self-help exercise on the following page, you can begin to understand how PMS can emotionally carry over from one generation to the next.

Take a Positive Approach

To keep history from repeating itself, talk to your daughter about the relationship between her body and her mind. She has a right to know about PMS and understand that it is a medical disorder that can be treated. Educate your daughter about PMS so that if she experiences PMS at some time during her life, she will not have to go through a questioning period of "What's wrong with me?" Rather, she will already be informed and will know what action to take.

Self-Help Exercise

MOM AND ME

1. Write a short biography of your mother, recording her emotions as you remember them. Did she have dramatic mood swings? Do you remember her as unpredictable? Did she cry a lot?
2. How do your mother's emotional characteristics compare to yours? How do/did you interact with your mother emotionally? How are you similar to and different from your mother?
3. If you have a teen-age daughter, describe how she is like/unlike you and your mother? Describe the times when the two of you are closest and the times when you are most distant emotionally.

If you are like other women who suffer from PMS, you will probably have mixed feelings about the knowledge that your mother had PMS. If your mother's PMS was severe, it may worry you to think that you will turn out like her. On the other hand, you most likely will think:

> *If only I had known what my mother was dealing with, I would have been much more tolerant and understanding . . . if only I had been told.*

When I hear this from women, I always sense some guilt about the past and some anxiety about the present. A woman who suffers from PMS can understandably be upset to think that her daughter might have to go through what she has gone through—both with herself and with you, her mother. Obviously no mother wants her child to suffer or feel guilty. We can talk to our daughters optimistically about the future in view of the fact that the body of information about PMS is rapidly expanding in both the medical and mental-health professions. For this reason, if your daughter does experience PMS, there will be less misunderstanding and confusion about the best treatment for her.

Synchronized Cycles

If you are living in the same house with your daughter, and your daughter has reached puberty, your cycles will probably become synchronized. This means that you and your daughter might be premenstrual at the same time. This can cause extra tension and anxiety. It can lead each of you to displace your own irritability onto the other. Justine, a 43-year-old woman with two teen-age children, said to me:

My 16-year-old daughter is very difficult to live with.

I suggested that she pay attention and discover if these "difficult-to-live-with" times occurred cyclically. I also suggested that if that was the case, her daughter probably found it difficult to live with her also!

Let your daughter know that the sooner (younger) she is treated for PMS, the fewer problems she will have. This can give her reassurance and confidence. The hope you give your daughter that she will not have to go through what you have is very positive. We can feel good about the idea that we can help our daughters rather than just feel sad for them.

Take a Positive Approach

You and your daughter can take a team approach to PMS. Make sure you are both taking the right vitamins, eating the right foods and exercising (all self-help measures discussed in Chapter 9). Have an understanding that if one of you says, "Give me room," the other knows that this is a clear signal and honors it.

CHAPTER 7

What Is He Thinking?

Men Talk About PMS

JIM'S STORY

She was the most vital and alive woman I have ever known. I don't know what changed. Every now and then, there is still some magic, but not enough to entice me back.

PMS chipped away at our relationship. Even though there was a reason for her amazing extremes, craziness and insulting behavior, it all hurt. Maybe she really couldn't control it, but did she have to be that harsh? She said shocking things. Ninety percent of what she said seemed insane, but 10% was true. I was confused with the duplicity of things she said. I didn't know what to believe.

I would come home at night and say, "Hi!" and her response would tell me how the rest of the evening would go. If she was in one of her moods, there was no safe place. She would bait me. Every statement would lead to an argument. And the arguments seemed constant, insignificant and neverending. I got to the point where I didn't care what the problem was or if there really was one. I couldn't stand it anymore. I thought I was going nuts.

I always had to be careful. There never seemed to be a time when we could calmly discuss the problem. It would have been very constructive to deal with the problem when we were more objective. At least that would have been a more rational approach. But when I asked her, "What is the best way to approach this?" I wouldn't get a straight answer.

It wore me down. I gradually retreated, becoming less com-

municative. I didn't like the person that I was becoming. After our arguments, I lost respect for myself. I'm a person who is used to being in control, but it made me feel powerless. I had to get away and put things in perspective. I needed distance.

We split up . . . sort of. We decided to live in separate places and see each other if it felt right for both of us. We are getting counseling, and she is getting medical treatment. But there is still a lot of the same old behavior . . . defense mechanisms on both sides. I called a week ago and she got really angry on the phone. Later she called back to apologize. Same old story. I realized I probably wouldn't live with her again.

THERE ARE THOSE TIMES

During counseling sessions and information seminars, I ask men, "When your partner is premenstrual, how does she seem to you?" They say she looks, sounds and acts differently when she's in one of her moods. Mark, 45, a psychiatrist, said this about the differences he sees in his wife Maureen:

> *She's bright, competent, imaginative, dynamic, and wonderful to be around when she is in her good phase. Then there are those times when, excuse me, she is a real bitch. She's argumentative, overly emotional, sarcastic, and the last person I want to be around. The differences are really confusing.*

Frank, who accompanied his wife, Sandy, to the the PMS Clinic, also mentioned the noticeable differences in the way she interacts with him when she is premenstrual. He said:

> *It's a cycle. Periodically there's no communication, and then she comes back around and starts talking to me again. The day of her period and several days afterward are wonderful. She is on top of the world—not only talking to me, but also bubbling over with happiness. I live for those days.*

Often men talk about how their partners do not seem to be the same person they once knew. Bob, a computer programmer who had been married to Gloria for 9 years before they divorced, said:

There was a feeling of sadness . . . sadness for the way we used to be. I guess it was a combination of both sadness and anger—not to mention confusion.

Bob felt sad, angry and confused—all at the same time. He felt like he had lost a good friend because it seemed to him that Gloria had become a different person than the woman he married.

HE NEEDS TO KNOW THAT PMS IS REAL

Typically, a man feels quite confused by a woman's PMS symptoms. He often absorbs some of her anxiety, irritability and depression. After counseling hundreds of men, I realize that men need accurate information regarding PMS and its effect on the relationship. They need information that validates that PMS is real, because there are so many messages out there that say it isn't. I believe that education is the best tool for dealing with PMS. For a couple to deal with the disorder effectively, both need to be well-informed and aware of each other's feelings.

In most of this chapter, I am addressing men. Then in the last part, I talk with both men and women. The man's perspective is preserved as much as possible in the first part of the chapter. Explanations may be included when they are helpful, but mostly men speak for themselves. This has two purposes. For the man whose partner suffers from PMS, it is helpful to hear what other men say about their experiences. For the woman who suffers from PMS, it is beneficial to hear things from her partner's perspective.

In the last part of this chapter, men and women talk about how they would like to see each other handle the problem. They both offer suggestions on how they would write the script for their interactions, if they could.

A Man's Positive Approach

The healthiest attitude toward PMS is to treat it as a medical disorder. It can cause mood changes that complicate your relationship. The situation requires your understanding and sympathy. Ideally, you are a significant support person for your partner. How can you be part of the solution?

- Tell her you want to help her.
- Try to remain objective enough to play a supportive role.
- Cultivate lots of patience.

WALKING ON EGGSHELLS

You probably notice that there are certain times when you have to be very careful not to do or say anything that will upset your wife or girlfriend. As J.D., a real estate broker who had been married to Diane for 7 years, said:

> *There are times when, no matter what I do, she becomes angry and baits me. It is almost as if she wants to have an argument or a fight. But it doesn't happen all the time. When I started paying attention to the timing, I realized that her mood changed around the time of her period. Then I realized that we were dealing with something on a regular basis.*

You might feel like saying to her, "Maybe your problems are associated with your period." But she's already angry, and no one can blame you for not wanting to make her angrier.

During those times, you probably find yourself staying off problem topics. Or, you might juggle things to keep peace in the family by making apologies to family and friends. In fact, you might do everything you can to control the situation so she is not antagonized. For example, if a bill comes that day, you make sure that she doesn't see it. You'll probably find, however, that a blowup can occur even when you are careful.

When you are making these efforts, you are probably taking on more than your share of responsibility for the relationship. This might be temporarily necessary, but it should not go on forever.

What About Me?

Often men tell me that they get more than a little irritated when confronted on a regular basis with an angry wife or lover. I have heard the following statement many, many times:

> *At the end of the day—often a rough one—I'm faced with an angry and cantankerous wife. I'm in no mood to have to handle her with kid gloves. In fact, I feel like I need a little extra attention and understanding. What about my needs?*

It seems as if you're having to take on an extra emotional responsibility, as well as figure out a way to keep peace at home. You're probably tired of it—understandably so.

Take a deep breath. Keep in mind that there are two problems here. One of them is her medical problem and the other is the way you're feeling. If you can keep these issues separate in your own mind, they will be more manageable. Each of these should be recognized and discussed.

When you return at the end of the day, it's best if you take a little time for yourself. This is your transition time to make the adjustment between work and home. Let her know that you're home and that you'll be able to spend time with her as soon as you have some time to recover and renew your energy. You might want to go for a jog or take a quick shower. Whatever you do, choose an activity you find relaxing and enjoyable so you can make the transition smoothly.

Sympathetic PMS

If you are typical of other men living with a woman who suffers from PMS, you are probably on an emotional roller coaster with her. Many men are concerned about the behavior they exhibit in response to her behavior—what I call *sympathetic PMS*. Sympathetic PMS happens when you respond to her anxiety with anxiety, anger with anger. Or it might be irritation, loss of patience, guilt, feelings that you are responsible for her situation (exactly what she has told you during an angry blowup). After hearing this often enough from her (once a month will do), you can begin to think that something is wrong with you. Dave, 40, a chemical engineer, put it this way:

> *After a while, I took it pretty personally, and I felt helpless to do anything but watch. If there's a solution and you avoid it, what does that show? I don't know. It was all so frustrating. Trying to identify something that was affecting both of us so much . . . God, it was a real horror story.*

PMS is a syndrome of extremes. For you—the partner of a woman suffering from PMS—going through PMS is much like what the partner of an alcoholic goes through. Roles change. In response to her PMS and in an attempt to relieve the tension, you might act out, try to become invisible, or become a clown. In other words, you might play a different role in the relationship than you normally would.

A Man's Positive Approach

You can demonstrate support for her by reading the literature on PMS, attending an information seminar on PMS or accompanying her to a PMS clinic. Your interest and presence tell her a lot—that you care and want to be supportive. She might not verbalize her awareness or her gratitude, but she will notice and appreciate your attention.

The Ping-Pong Effect

There is a tendency when a woman suffers from PMS for emotions to bounce back and forth between the man and the woman. Here's what I mean.

She gets angry and unloads on you by making some caustic remarks, for example. You feel cut to the quick. Then her period comes, and she starts feeling better. At this point, she may come to you as if nothing ever happened. This probably surprises and confuses you because you are still feeling upset and angry about what took place. You're not feeling particularly forgiving, and it's probably going to take you a while to get over the angry incident.

The irony of this situation is that now that she's feeling better, you're feeling angry and hurt. Just about the time you start feeling better and get over your anger, it's time for PMS to begin again. I call this the ping-pong effect: the anger and hurt bounces back and forth between you.

Ultimately, PMS can feel like the controlling factor in the relationship. Ed, a photographer with a family of three, described how it seemed that PMS controlled the relationship with his wife, Mary:

> *Our social life would drive me crazy. At a party she would become very jealous. Really, for no apparent reason. After a while, I refused to go to any parties with her. We see fewer friends now. I found myself making excuses when she didn't feel like going out. After a while, our friends stopped calling. It was hard on me. Her too. You know, you kind of feel isolated, which doesn't help things. We even stopped going out for dinner much. Why should we go and spend all that money if all she wants to do is either argue all night or be depressed? Great choices for me!*

A Man's Positive Approach

Create healthy diversions when she is premenstrual. If she is upset, ask her to go for a walk with you. If she is fatigued from caring for the children, suggest that she take a bubble bath while you take over. If you are working together on a Saturday project, suggest a break and fix a snack rather than working straight through. The best way to be supportive is through your actions. It's the little things that count.

The Mushroom Cloud Goes Up

When a woman becomes angry, aggressive and hostile, how do you perceive her behavior? Bob vividly described his wife Carolyn's behavior and how he feared for their children. He said:

> *She would put an amazing amount of energy into our fights. Sometimes she really looked like a mad woman. Sorry, but there's just no other way to describe it. She would rip clothes out of the closet and throw things. I could see the fear in our kids' eyes. I know that feeling because I felt it myself. When she'd go crazy like this, I felt afraid because there was no telling what might happen next.*

A woman's premenstrual behavior can evoke a mixture of emotions that include confusion, apprehension and fear. Often you may think:

> *I feel threatened when she comes after me.*

> *I'd rather be taking care of myself.*

One of your impulses is to defend yourself, but at the same time you probably feel confused and wonder if you should be protecting her. You probably don't know what to do. Should you defend yourself? Should you try to calm her down? Should you ignore her? You might wonder:

> *What does she need? She seems so upset and yet I can't figure out what she wants or needs.*

To some extent, you are absorbing her ambivalence. In reaction to her angry outburst, you are probably thinking you need to take care of yourself—but you can't walk out the door. Why? Well, what about her? It probably doesn't feel comfortable to leave her alone. On the other hand, it doesn't feel emotionally safe for you to stay.

Beware! It is very easy for you to absorb her anger and hostility. It seems as if she knows exactly what to do and say to make you angry. You become upset because her behavior seems so dramatic.

When she becomes angry, try to not see it as directed toward you. Allow for the fact that her anger can be a result of PMS. It might be difficult for you to stay detached from her anger, but it is crucial to do so. It is the only healthy approach. If you become entangled and angry yourself, the situation can escalate quickly and get out of control. This is a no-win situation because she is unlikely to let go of her anger.

If you have been living with PMS bouts for a long time, you have probably felt the following emotions that men have described to me in counseling sessions:

• *She acts irrational.* She becomes argumentative, emotional, irrational and paranoid.

• *I'm the cause of all her problems.* Sometimes I feel like I'm her whipping post. No matter what happens, I'm to blame.

• *She won't fight fair.* When we argue, I keep from saying anything destructive. But not her. She goes for the throat. She says everything that she can to wound me. Every time something goes wrong, she threatens—screams—that she is leaving. She uses as ammunition against me the very things that I tell her in confidence. It makes me furious to hear these things used against me. If I can't confide in her, who can I confide in?

• *It's really confusing.* She wants her own space, but she wants nurturing too. She'll say, "Get out of here." But if I leave, there's hell to pay. My response to her is usually, "What do you want me to do? Do you want me to stay or go? If you want me to go, I'll go. If you want me to stay, I'll stay. But right now I don't have the slightest idea what you want." She's confused, and she makes me confused. I'm just tired of the yo-yo act.

• *I don't believe her.* She keeps saying that there is something wrong with her, but the doctors say there's nothing wrong with her. I believe the doctors—all three of them. They keep telling her she's fine, so sure I'm skeptical. I mean, they should know, shouldn't they?

• *I'm afraid.* I'm afraid of her highs because it means that her lows are going to be equally dramatic. PMS scares the hell out of me! I'm afraid to say what I really think when she's in one of her moods. The smallest thing can set off an explosion. I'm afraid that her PMS will mean the end of our relationship.

• *It's so frustrating.* It took a lot of time . . . more than a year . . . to convince her to go for help. Then watching her refuse to follow through, I feel as if she wanted us to fail. Even now, it sometimes seems to me that she wants to destroy us.

• *It's ruining our relationship.* After one of those huge fights, neither sex, nor hugs nor kisses can make up for the lack of trust I feel. I just know that our relationship is deteriorating.

SEXUAL DYNAMICS OF PMS

A man typically says that what he would like in a relationship is a close friend and companion. He wants to be able to give and receive emotional support from someone with whom he feels unguarded, relaxed and psychologically secure. He also wants a lover, someone with whom he can be physically close, intimate, sharing, nurturing and protective. However, these are the very aspects of a relationship that become jeopardized when she is premenstrual.

According to research carried out at the PMS Clinic, low sex drive is definitely an issue with PMS for both men and women. A woman will say:

> *I don't understand it. I used to feel like a normal sexual human being, but now I'm finding I have very little or no sex drive. My husband is hurt by this, and I'm not pleased with the situation myself.*

Some of the literature about PMS suggests that low sex drive is not a problem. It is often reported that a woman feels a heightened sex drive throughout her premenstrual phase. However, the overwhelming majority of women who have sought counseling at the PMS Clinic report that their sex drive usually decreases when they are premenstrual. Some say that if their sex drive is present when they are premenstrual, it is very strong but short-lived. This is another one of the extremes associated with PMS that presents a significant problem for a couple's relationship.

It is clearly an area where you can feel a lot of rejection. Bob, married to Nancy for 13 years, said:

> *That's just one more disagreement that my wife and I have. I feel rejected when she doesn't want to be sexual.*

A Man's Positive Approach

Your emotions are genuine and need to be validated. Express what you are thinking and feeling, because she needs to hear your side of the story. She will be most receptive if you initiate a discussion during a time when she doesn't have PMS. If you feel that you don't have a forum in which to express your thoughts, it is probably time to contact a counselor. It will help open up communications. Your partner will appreciate your concern and most likely respond positively. She probably feels confused and would like to express her feelings too. It's a good idea to have a designated place and time in which to do this with a third party who can mediate.

He Feels Rejected

When your lover is cold and aloof, how does this make you feel? You might feel a lack of emotional support and understanding, and that your intimate life with her is fading. You probably feel the same way that other men have expressed in the following ways:

- *I become confused.* Is the change in her sexual behavior due to hormones? Or, is the reason that she doesn't want to make love because her breasts hurt? Or, is the reason because she is in such a bad mood . . . so angry that she baits me into getting into a fight . . . then no one wants to make love, including me?

- *I don't believe her.* I don't accept her story that her feelings about sex are so different at different times. I find it hard to believe that she can be so sexual during part of the month and so non-sexual at other times.

- *I think that something is wrong with me.* I assume that if she rejects me some of the time and not all the time there must be something that I'm doing to upset her.

- *I think that our intimate relationship is "wearing out"—that we are falling out of love.* I get the feeling that no matter how I respond to her criticisms it doesn't matter. Why? Because she doesn't really love me any more, that's why. I'm convinced of it. If we fight instead of making love, it tells me that there's something fundamentally wrong with the relationship.

- *I feel manipulated.* She is either very sexual or very non-sexual. It feels like she's manipulating me. Of course, I take it very personally.

The issue of sex is clearly an area where her behavior can seem quite manipulative to you. For example, if she sets the stage—fixes a candlelight dinner for you—and then changes her mind at the last minute, her sudden change of mood can confuse you and make you feel rejected. She probably becomes angry with herself and feels guilty. Then you both feel frustrated.

A Man's Positive Approach

Keep your expectations realistic about what you can do. Try not to become discouraged when your efforts to help don't seem to make a difference. On some level she is aware of and appreciates your efforts. Remind yourself that things will improve with treatment.

Hormonal imbalances create changes in sex drive. You need to be aware of this. This is not directed at you, even though it may feel like it is. Talk with her about how you feel. If the situation has deteriorated significantly, perhaps the two of you can agree to initiate some professional counseling around this issue.

HIS SELF-ESTEEM SUFFERS TOO

When your wife or girlfriend is physically or emotionally down, you probably want to do what you can to help. During her PMS time, however, when she is down and you try to help out, you might not be able to figure out how to make her feel better. Graham, an artist, expressed his dilemma this way:

> *I feel inadequate and ineffective. It's like I can't do anything to help. Everything I do seems wrong.*

In other words, whether Graham helped or not didn't seem to make any difference in her attitude. You might also feel "damned if you do and damned if you don't."

Have you ever asked her what you could do to help, and had her answer through clenched teeth, "If I knew, don't you think I'd tell you?" If so, you probably felt ineffective and frustrated. On the other hand, she probably felt guilty because she pushed you away when you were trying to help.

To further confuse the issue, she may sometimes give you mixed messages when you try to help. She may say she needs nurturing and closeness at the same time that she says she needs space and distance. It can leave you in a quandary when she says, "I want space—leave me alone," and soon follows it with, "You better not leave." She's telling you she wants two opposite things!

You want her to make herself clear. However, she cannot tell you what she wants or needs when she doesn't know either. It might help you to realize that her conflict is similar to that of a person who wants to go swimming, but doesn't want to get wet.

A Man's Positive Approach

Because this is a stressful time for you, do something positive for yourself. Exercise on a regular basis can be especially helpful. This helps relieve your stress so you can feel better about yourself and keep your perspective.

Both of her needs—the need for distance and the need for closeness—are valid. The problem is that they can't be accomplished at the same time.

It's easy to see how you can feel confused and ineffective in this situation. What can you do when she sends you mixed messages? First, recognize that she is as confused as you are—but it won't be this way forever. Once the medical problem is resolved, the rest will fall into place. Second, there are times when no matter what you say or do to help, she may become upset anyway. Once you have done your best, don't blame yourself for not being able to solve the problem.

No man wants a partner who is "not OK" and who consequently makes him feel "not OK." All of us want things to get back to normal. But the situation that has developed due to PMS can make you question everything about yourself. After telling me that his partner seemed "crazed" to him, Dick, a sales representative, asked me:

> *If I stay with her, is this an indication of my love, my stupidity, or my masochism?*

His sense of self had clearly been jeopardized.

Unfortunately, it can be easy for you to absorb some of her dissatisfaction with the world and begin to feel confused and guilty yourself. Almost inevitably, your self-esteem begins to be negatively affected. When this happens, it can be hard to sympathize with her. Additionally, because you feel victimized, there are now two PMS victims instead of one!

RECOVERING THE RELATIONSHIP

If you have been dealing with your partner's premenstrual behavior for a long time, it is an exciting and hopeful time when she begins to get help. You will probably be very happy to think that there is treatment for the problem. Most men are.

Sheila and Dave, a couple in their early forties, have been married for 22 years. Dave accompanied her to the PMS Clinic when she began treatment. He participated in the information seminars for men, as well, and spoke up to say:

> *I was elated! For me to think that there was help for what she and I were going through . . . I was so happy. Now that we know what it is, it's obvious that PMS has been affecting our relationship for years.*

It was important for him to know that she was taking some responsibility for getting better. He felt more motivated to help her once she was willing to take some initial steps. When she started to help herself, this also gave him cues about how he could help her.

The Relationship Can Change

Often a man will report that when his wife or lover starts to get better, the dynamics of their relationship change. You might also feel this change. For example, when she is regaining control, you might feel less needed. As a result, you might suffer feelings of inadequacy without knowing why. This kind of dynamic is sometimes seen in cases of alcoholism where, once the dependent person overcomes the problem, the partner becomes lost and confused. Even though the alcoholic person is no longer drinking, the couple has established behavioral styles that do not automatically go away. So, while one person is putting the pieces together again, the other is feeling left out.

This dynamic suggests another slant on sympathetic PMS. Sympathetic PMS is what my husband suffered from when, 2 months after I had started effectively treating my PMS and was doing very well, he said, "You've gotten rid of PMS. Now I think I have it!" The two of us discussed it. He meant that he had developed survival techniques in response to my premenstrual behavior. These were necessary in order to live with me. Now he was noticing that my behavior was changing. How was he going to change his? He said he felt like he didn't fit into the picture any longer and that he had somehow been replaced. He said he liked the fact that I had gotten better, but it had changed the relationship. It left him feeling confused and not knowing what to do.

Another important point is that a woman who is recovering from PMS will tend to take over responsibility for the problem. In fact, she might see herself as being responsible for all the problems that have developed in the relationship, and be tempted to say, "It's all my fault."

It would be easy for you to let her take all the blame, but this isn't a good idea. It prevents you from getting the relationship back on track. There should be equal concern and responsibility.

A Man's Positive Approach

Be sensitive to the situation by focusing on what needs to be done. Being sensitive does not mean being a "helicopter husband" who hovers over her. It does mean figuring out what needs to be done—and doing it. Don't wait for her to say, "This is what needs to be done." If the kids need to eat, feed them. If the baby needs to be changed, change him.

Together, the Two of You Can Make It

When each person in the relationship understands and appreciates what the other has gone though as a result of PMS, it can bring the couple closer together. Roger, married to Teresa for 15 years, participated in the PMS Clinic's information seminars for men. He said:

> *Now that PMS is controlled, I know that going through the experience together helped strengthen our relationship. It was the ultimate test and we made it. There was a sense of appreciation from both of us. She appreciated the fact that I was supportive and non-judgmental. I admired her for her determination to help herself, and as a result, to help our family. I guess you would call it a bonding effect.*

The following checkpoints are important steps in this recovery process.

✔ *Build a Bridge*

Communication is crucial. Communication is the way to build a bridge. This does not mean the woman says she is to blame, or the man says he is somehow responsible for the problem. Rather, both are encouraged to talk so each person feels that he or she is part of the solution, not just part of the problem.

✔ *Set Up a Forum*

During the recovery stage, both partners need to acknowledge the need for a forum—a designated time and place—to discuss what is happening. This is how they would discuss any problem (medical or otherwise) that affected their relationship. If PMS is discussed in a timely fashion, the man will usually heave a sigh of relief when

A Man's Positive Approach

Take some time to talk with her about negative behaviors you may have developed in response to her PMS. How did you see yourself fitting into the picture in the past? How do you see yourself fitting into the picture now? How do you see yourself fitting into the picture in the future? This kind of soul-searching can be difficult but invaluable in trying to make your relationship more positive.

the woman lets him know that her needs are confusing to her, so they must be confusing to him as well. Recognizing that there are no easy answers is important for both partners. Because both are working on the problem, they are showing each other that they can make a joint effort. This is positive and can strengthen the relationship.

✔ *Air Your Gripes*

Emotions that build up can cause resentment and anger that is very destructive. To ensure that this doesn't happen, you must learn to air your gripes before they grow into large problems. The exercises on the following pages can help each partner begin to do this.

✔ *Learn the Best Way to Talk With Each Other*

Each person needs to take responsibility for expressing what is going on with him or her emotionally in the most loving and clear manner possible. If you feel confused, acknowledge this. If you feel incapable of making decisions, tell your partner. Express what you need—no matter how selfish it sounds to you. For example, the woman might say:

> *I need you to be more understanding. I can be up one moment and down the next. I need you to be sensitive to my changing moods. I'm sorry I seem so up and down, but if you're understanding of it, it helps me feel more balanced.*

Additionally, she should be as clear and specific as possible about her needs. She could say, for example:

> *I want you to be close, but not too close. I want you to call me from work, but not until later in the afternoon.*

He might say to her:

> *If you're headed for your PMS time, let me know specifically how I can help out at home. If you'd like me to plan on cooking that week, that's something I'd like to do. The important thing is that you let me know, because I'm not a mind-reader.*

Tell Her How You'd Write the Script

At information seminars for men held at the PMS Clinic, men were asked how they would change PMS scenarios if they could. Here are some typical responses:

- *We would have signals about what mood she was in.* When I'd come home, there would be a signal on the refrigerator door. When the signal was on, it would be my indicator that there was trouble—big trouble! If I could write the script, I'd tell her to mellow out, and she would actually listen to me and do it!

- *I wouldn't discuss anything of importance during her PMS time*. It seems as though everything that is said at that time is so damaging, and it erodes the foundation of our relationship. If I could write the script, I'd have it so we could talk openly about our relationship when she's feeling OK.

- *I would want PMS to be fixed like any other medical problem.* If I could write the script, there wouldn't be all this mystery around the problem. It would be considered more treatable and more manageable.

Tell Him How You'd Write the Script

When I ask women how they would ideally choose to have their partners deal with the situation, I receive many candid responses and good ideas about taking a positive approach to PMS. Following are some of the suggestions from women:

- *Let's talk it over*. Together we can work it out, but to do that, we need to validate and appreciate what each other has gone through and talk about it empathetically.

A Man's Positive Approach

Tell her that you appreciate what she is going through and that you support her. For example, you can say:

- *It's really good to see that you are getting help and helping yourself.*
- *I appreciate it when you ask me to help you through this process.*
- *I like it when you talk with the kids about what is happening.*
- *I know it's not easy, but I'm optimistic about the future.*

• *Let's take a look at the calendar.* If I get mad, don't think that I hate you . . . don't jump to the conclusion that our marriage is on the rocks. If we keep a calendar, it's very clear to both of us when the problem is caused by my cycle. This way, you will understand that it's the time of the month rather than thinking that there is something terribly wrong with our relationship. If I acknowledge this to you, it calms me down and I'm less likely to direct my anger at you.

• *Let's keep the right perspective.* I need you as a support person. It's not going to do either one of us any good if you absorb the anger and let me antagonize you. If I do get angry, please don't get in the car and take off. It just makes the problem worse. Because of PMS, my anger is there whether you are or not. You are not necessarily the source of my anger when I'm premenstrual.

• *Let's mend our fences.* There are things I would like to talk to you about—things that have taken place in the past. For example, I really blew up at the kids recently and this worried you a lot. By looking back at the calendar, I can see that it happened the day before my period. Let's talk about it now.

• *Could you accompany me when I go to the clinic?* I very much want you to know what I'm going through. I think that this might be a relief for you too. I know that it would give us—as a couple—a really different attitude toward PMS.

A Woman's Positive Approach

Tell him that you appreciate what he is going through and that it means a lot to have his support. For example, you can say:

• *You are really helping me by being supportive. I can deal with it so much more easily.*

• *I appreciate it when you take charge of what needs to be done at home without me having to ask you.*

• *I like it when you talk with the kids about what is happening with me.*

• *I know it's not easy, but I'm optimistic about the future.*

Self-Help Exercise for Him

HE WISHES HE COULD TELL HER . . .

- *Just say it (don't scream it)!*
- *You can't have it both ways. If you don't want me here, I don't want to be here.*
- *I need to be a partner in this process, not a victim of it. We need to make conquering PMS a common goal.*
- *Please don't assume that I can read your mind. Talk to me about what's going on.*
- *I would like to keep a chart of our fights. Then I would like to take a look at the pattern with you. We also need to have rules for fair fighting.*
- *It is really important for me to see you take responsibility and try to get better.*
- *I have a legitimate reason to gripe if you are not doing the things that you need to do to take care of yourself and get better.*
- *Just because you are unhappy doesn't mean that I have to be unhappy. If you want to withdraw, that's fine. I want to be supportive, but I don't want to feel like I have to withdraw.*
- ____
- ____
- ____
- ____

Self-Help Exercise for Her

SHE WISHES SHE COULD TELL HIM . . .

- *Tune into what's going on and what needs to be done.*
- *Don't treat me like I'm crazy.*
- *Don't use PMS as an excuse for not listening to me or for not taking me seriously.*
- *Be aware of when I'm headed into my bad times.*
-
-
-
-
-
-

CHAPTER 8

CAREER CONCERNS:
PMS and Your Work

SUE'S STORY

I have my career. I have my freedom and independence. I also have my family. So why do I become depressed and irritable all of a sudden? I tend to blame it on my job.

I've been a flight attendant for a major airline for 16 years. Mine is a high-profile job: face-to-face with people who pay for and are entitled to good service. To make sure that they get it, my supervisors "ghost ride." So when a passenger or the pilot starts making demands that would strain anybody's nerves, I've got to keep cool. I can't say, "You know, it's the day before my period, and you're getting on my nerves." I become an actress and pretend that whatever the passenger says or does is OK. Then I go back to the galley and start slamming around everything in sight, upsetting the other attendants who are trying to prepare about 100 dinners in a space the size of a small bathroom!

I'm also the union representative for 1400 flight attendants in our company. I defend a lot of women in their thirties who have PMS and don't know it. I show them the literature on PMS from our employee assistance program. We talk about how our work conditions exacerbate PMS: the altitude, the processed food, the pressure in the cabin, and the sleep that we don't get because of our schedules.

If the flight attendant knows about PMS, she can see how different the same flights to the same city can be at different times of the month. One week everything is fine. The next week is OK. The third week is when she starts banging things around in the galley. By the fourth week, she's premenstrual and ready to explode. Most of the time, she can hide it or put on an act; but by the end of her cycle it's incredibly difficult.

The one hopeful thought I hang onto is that the good time is as predictable as the bad time.

WHAT WORKING WOMAN ISN'T AFFECTED?

With women having dual roles more than at any time in history, the pressures of PMS can manifest themselves in ways different from the past. We are more visible now—out there in the work force, as well as working at home. Here's what working women in different occupations have told me about their experiences during their PMS time:

A Waitress:

I'm a waitress. I dread those days. I carry only half-full trays.

A Secretary:

I have a desk job, and all I do is push papers around on those days.

A Lawyer:

I'm a lawyer—and a good one. However, occasionally I have asked for an extension when I knew that my mind would not be sharp enough to prepare a strong case for my client. I guess that is "copping out." I rationalize and say that I'm doing my client a favor.

A Housewife:

None of the housework gets done, and I feel like running away from my kids during that time.

A Writer:

I worked on my first book during my good times only. So I spent 2 years writing it instead of one!

A Nurse:

I'm real worried about giving the wrong medication on those days. I double- and triple-check myself.

A Teacher:

The noise in the classroom during that time of the month is overwhelming. It really strains my patience. Those are the days when I can't stand the kids.

A Technician:

Coordination in precision work is very difficult for me during that time of the month.

A Doctor:

As a physician, I have to be responsible all *the time. Sometimes I look at the hospital orders that I gave when I was premenstrual, and I can't believe I wrote them!*

The results of our research at the PMS Clinic show that women perceive that PMS significantly affects their work in the following ways:

- 94% reported that PMS negatively affects their job performance.
- 92% reported that they would be more productive in their professional lives if they did not have PMS.

Body Time and Work Time

A job typically requires that you be there every day that you're scheduled to work. You must be punctual, look presentable, think clearly, interact and communicate with other people in a professional way, deal with problems and complex situations, and act decisively. However, when your body "betrays" you (as many women report) and prevents you from working efficiently, tension is created. A lot of energy can be expended just putting one foot in front of the other.

Your body time may not equate with work time. You may not feel like going to work. You may be late for work. You might think that you look terrible. You might feel confused and dazed. You might want to isolate yourself and not interact with other people. You might feel like you can't cope with problems that are out of the ordinary. And you might feel like you can't act decisively.

It is important to remember that everyone—every man and every woman—has experienced each one of these feelings at some time or another. Everyone has temporary interruptions in work due to physical and psychological problems. Men may experience similar feelings. However, they may not be as obvious because they don't form a noticeable pattern. Rather, they occur randomly.

The woman who suffers from PMS does so on a temporary basis, but it can overlap with all of her work life. It can be more difficult for her because she is working harder to achieve her goals than she would be if she weren't suffering from PMS. She has usually developed additional self-discipline and coping techniques that help her get her work done despite the problem. Once she begins to get PMS under control, she usually finds that she has more energy than she realized. This helps in developing good work habits that enable her to accomplish what she desires.

In this chapter, we are going to take a look at the different ways in which PMS can affect us in the workplace. We are also going to look at an interesting phenomenon. Many professional women report that, just at the point when they are about to move ahead in their careers, they feel that doors begin to close. They attribute this to their PMS. Even more interesting is the fact that once these women have gained control of PMS, they report feeling once again that "the sky's the limit." They say they have the energy and desire to achieve goals they set earlier in their careers. There are many reports from women who at one time felt pessimistic about how PMS was affecting their work life. However, they have used the information they have gained about themselves while treating PMS and have gone on to achieve their goals.

Finally, in this chapter we are going to address some issues from an employer's perspective. Today there are many enlightened men and women in the business world in decision-making positions who would like to know what measures can be taken to help women in the work force who suffer from PMS.

Your State of Mind Affects Your Work

Today's economy is an information economy. The typical workplace is made up of "knowledge workers" whose skills are mostly intellectual, not manual. What is the effect of PMS when your mind (your major work tool) is dulled and confused? Teresa, 34, a high-school teacher, reported:

> *I can't think straight. I have problems remembering. Sometimes it feels like I have syrup around my brain. It's difficult to be clear with my students on those days.*

When you are premenstrual, your state of mind is negatively affected and your work life can suffer as a result. To say, "I'm not me at that time of the month" means that you may have difficulty working at the same level of proficiency that you normally do. Women often report difficulty coping with routine jobs when they are premenstrual, and they say they feel like they are present at work in the physical sense only. The problem is that women who are premenstrual are often feeling off balance in the physical sense also.

Remember that even though you may be less tolerant of your errors, you probably are perceiving them as bigger than they really are. Try to keep your perspective and realize that you put the typewriter ribbon in backwards last week and it didn't seem like such a big problem. In other words, the problem didn't change—your perspective did. Try not to blow things out of proportion.

PMS can create or contribute to an almost compulsive sense of drive. At the same time, you are likely to be more critical of yourself. It's a good idea not to become so immersed in the problem that you feel like you can't do anything about it. Don't trap yourself.

Your Body's Condition Can Make it Hard to Work Too

The physical symptoms of PMS that interfere most with work include:

- Backaches
- Migraine headaches
- Joint aches and pains
- Sluggishness, fatigue and exhaustion

Women report feeling so sluggish and fatigued when they are premenstrual that even routine tasks seem like major hurdles. During that time of the month, many say they often go back to work at night to finish a regular day's work.

Headaches are a common complaint. When women are premenstrual, many have migraine headaches of such severity that it is difficult for them to work. Women often mention that they go on "automatic pilot" when they are premenstrual—which means that routine tasks are carried out, but extras don't get done.

The outcome of PMS might be that you have to work harder—at the very time when you feel like you have more work than you can handle. As Ruth, 33, an accountant, pointed out:

> *My tapes don't balance, my invoices don't balance. The next day I have to try to find the mistakes. Sometimes I think it is going to be impossible to keep my job.*

Take a Positive Approach

When you are having difficulty coping, lower your expectations. Give yourself permission to take care of yourself. Don't schedule extra work during difficult days. Take more frequent breaks. When the day is over, give yourself credit for having accomplished a full day's work.

The stress and tension that PMS creates begin to compound. You may begin to worry about what your employer thinks, or whether your performance will negatively affect your promotion. Many women mention that they cross their fingers on those days, hoping that nothing stressful will come up because they can't deal with it.

Working with the Public

Many jobs require that you be polite, project yourself and sell. It can be especially difficult to meet and greet the public when you are premenstrual. It is the time when you are most likely to feel apologetic, depressed, moody and withdrawn. Due to lack of self-confidence, you might think you come across to the public as unprofessional.

The low self-esteem that is a natural by-product of PMS can negatively affect your communication skills and the image other people have of you. As different women have reported:

> *My nervousness influences my relations with the public. At that time of the month, I can't be confident about the products that I sell.*

> *Business relationships can really be jeopardized. It's difficult to negotiate a contract when I feel so insecure.*

Women often talk about putting on an act to sound professional. Interestingly enough, they usually carry it off fairly well. Just as the flight attendant's story at the beginning of this story relates, making it through the tough times is difficult—but possible. Most of us do it quite well. Having PMS requires a lot of energy, and working during those times places more demands on our energy levels. It is essential to add to that energy level in any way we can while we work on getting PMS under control. We must give ourselves permission to take good care of ourselves on those days. The ups of PMS are as predictable as the downs, so as you get PMS more under control, the downs will be milder and fewer while the up time will happen more often.

Take a Positive Approach

Lighten up. Look for constructive ways to relieve the tension. For a change of scenery, walk downstairs to another office during your coffee break. To escape the noise in your office at lunchtime, change your clothes and go for a run.

Your Self-Image

When you are premenstrual, you are likely to feel that your hair looks limp, your body looks fat and frumpy, and your complexion is a mess. You might feel that your face looks like a teen-ager's. Probably the last thing that you want to do is greet the public. As Sarah, 39, a lawyer and mother of a 2-year old, said:

> *My confidence level about the way I project is at an all-time low. I make sure that court dates are set for another time.*

Keep in mind that you are probably more self-conscious during your premenstrual time. Remind yourself often that your perceptions of yourself are different than others'. You probably have an exaggerated sense of ineptitude or lack of a good image. Of course, this doesn't mean that other people see you this way.

Notice also what Sarah did to take care of herself professionally. She made sure that important dates were scheduled for another time. This may seem as if you are scheduling your work according to your body's calendar, but it is probably temporary. You are actively working on getting PMS under control, and most likely you won't have to reorganize your schedule much longer to allow for this.

Work Conditions Can Exacerbate PMS

The physical and psychological symptoms of PMS can be exacerbated by workplace conditions. Noise is a major factor, including the noise of typewriters, phones or printers, factory noise, and the noise of children and toddlers. Christine, 32, an administrative assistant for a major corporation, told me:

> *The sound of typewriters, phones and computers makes me crazy. I can't stand the noise. It makes my nerves jangle so much that I feel I'm going to jump out of my skin.*

Take a Positive Approach

Do you have favorite outfits? During your PMS time, wear clothes that you feel best in—ones in which you feel most comfortable and least self-conscious. Dress so that you don't have to worry about how you look. Use your clothes to give you a lift.

Many other work conditions exacerbate PMS. Flight attendants report being negatively affected by high altitude and cabin pressure when they are premenstrual. Eating hurriedly and working night shifts or split shifts—standard fare in many lines of work—seriously affect the worker who has PMS. Night-shift work is especially hard on PMS sufferers because it upsets the body's natural cycle and can lead to depression.

You May Need to Take Some Precautions

The U.S. Center for Safety Education has found that the two-day period before the onset of menstruation is the time when accidents at work are most likely to occur for a woman. Carelessness, clumsiness, and lowered physical coordination can be quite dangerous, as 29-year-old Melodie, a delivery person, suggested:

> *My job includes driving. Do you know how dangerous driving is at that time of the month? Sometimes I can't remember how I got to a place.*

It is obviously important—if for no other reason than physical safety—that you recognize your limits. You might need to discuss the problem with your employer or a co-worker. It is preferable to ask for understanding than to say nothing and risk having an accident.

Switching to other possible areas of work during this time is one way of dealing with the situation. For example, if you work in a floral shop and normally you deliver orders, consider taking orders over the phone instead for a day or two. Do whatever you can to avoid overextending yourself. Make sure to take some breaks during the day. Everyone needs them, not just women who have PMS. Most companies give their employees break times because workers are more attentive and productive after breaks. Allow the same for yourself—for the same reason.

Take a Positive Approach

Planning is control. Don't rely on luck to keep stressful events at work from occurring while you are premenstrual. Try to anticipate times when you will be under extra stress and tension. Whenever possible, schedule your calendar so you can deal with the extra stress when you are best able to do so.

SOCIAL DYNAMICS AT THE WORKPLACE

Even if your job does not require that you meet the public, most likely it requires that you interact professionally with your co-workers. If you are like other women who suffer from PMS, you can feel confused, temperamental, anti-social, and unresponsive when you are premenstrual. This can deplete your energy, making it harder for you (and your co-workers) to get the job done. As, Joanne, 36, a systems analyst, said:

> *At that time of the month, my perspective regarding people and situations is slanted.*

You may have either of two typical reactions to PMS. You may become angry and confront others or become sullen and hide out from others. If you become confrontational, you will probably find that this is when molehills grow into mountains. You might find yourself criticizing others and snapping at them. You might even become angry enough to explode. Lisa, 34, a secretary, described an angry outburst:

> *I just lost it. I screamed at my boss in front of everyone.*

In other words, PMS can take over the situation. Does this sound familiar? This is the same kind of explosion that you can have at home with your partner. At the workplace, however, there may be much less understanding and tolerance.

On the other hand, if you become sullen and withdraw, you are likely to stay away from everybody and become silently tearful. You may think you are protecting others from your behavior. What you are actually doing is building a wall around yourself as a survival strategy. You are conserving your energy so you can carry out your regular work.

Take a Positive Approach

To cope with fatigue, plan to get extra sleep when you are premenstrual. Go to bed a little earlier—especially if you have to work an irregular shift. Take cat-naps. Or, ask your family to help you by keeping the house quiet so you can lie down for 20 minutes before dinner.

Having PMS drains an amazing amount of energy. I compare it to being thrown in the middle of the ocean with no lifeboats in sight. You can tread water, but you can't swim. This is a good way to think of PMS when you are trying to figure out why you are detached from co-workers. When we have to use so much energy dealing with PMS, we are unlikely to want to interact with others because interacting requires energy. This pattern usually develops without us being aware of it. Only belatedly does it dawn on us that we have disconnected ourselves from others.

It is important to realize that you have choices about this. You can decide to reconnect or not reconnect with co-workers. What is crucial to realize is that previously PMS may have been making the choices for you. Now that you have started to regain control, you can make the choice.

How Does PMS Affect Your Status at Work?

If you are a working woman who suffers from PMS to such a degree that it interferes with your work, you may be nervous about the status of your job. PMS can affect your chances of getting a job, keeping it or receiving a promotion. Your anxiety about your job is understandable. Women often report:

> *I wake up in a panic that I can't do the work.*

The time when you are most likely to walk out impulsively is during your premenstrual phase (just as it is the time that you are most likely to walk out of your relationship). You are sure that anything would be better than the job (or relationship) that you are in. As Elizabeth, 39, a public relations specialist, said:

> *The only time that I have quit a job is before my period. Otherwise I usually figure out a solution that will work.*

Take a Positive Approach

Ask for the understanding and support of your co-workers. They would prefer to be asked for a little extra patience with you than to find themselves in an unexpected confrontation with you over something minor.

PMS is a temporary hurdle. It should not be allowed to get in the way of well-thought-out career plans. Bolster yourself with this thought as you continue to find effective ways to deal with PMS. Issues that have been accumulating—but have been manageable up to this point—now may seem overwhelming. Many women report giving up their hopes of a successful career when they are premenstrual. This is very unfortunate, because PMS is a temporary and treatable problem.

CONFLICTS BETWEEN PROFESSIONAL AND PERSONAL LIFE

If you have PMS, it can be very difficult for you to balance the private and professional areas of your life. Pressures and tensions in one area tend to spill over into the other. You might feel that you are on a treadmill, trying to catch up in one area—only to find that you have fallen behind in the other.

The stress of dual roles is so well known that many working women consider it a fact of life. For the woman who suffers from PMS, the stress can seem incredible. Many report that they want to give up work, abandoning the career goals they set out so earnestly to achieve. Suzanne, 41, a woman who owns a successful business, said to me:

> *I wish I wasn't a career person—I want to be a homemaker. I don't want to take the risks of being in the work world any longer. I wish I could just hide out at home and only have one job.*

If you are like many other women with PMS, you probably feel that you can manage your work at home well enough, but you cannot also manage your career at the same time. Your job or career seems to be a huge energy drain on you. You probably think, "If I spend my energy at work, what will I have left for my family?"

It takes extra energy to make it through the work day when you are premenstrual. Even if you manage to do so, you will probably find that the smallest thing can set you off once you get home from work. As Sue, 31, a security worker, said:

> *I keep it together at work—barely. Then I get home and bang! I explode. The next day I'm dragging, not just because I have low energy, but also because I feel so guilty about what happened at home.*

It can become extremely difficult to balance your public and private lives. In public, you hide. In private, you lose control. One part of life creates tension and anxiety about the other.

It is imperative that we see the interaction that takes place and use our support system to help us over the rough spots. There is nothing wrong with asking for extra assistance at home during a particularly stressful work week. Alleviating some homefront pressures can go a long way in reducing the sense of stress at work.

You Become a Super Secretary, A Super Lawyer, a . . .

If PMS has caused you to have a sporadic work record, you are likely to become quite anxious about your job. You may try to overcompensate during your good time by attempting to make up for any work you have lost. A sense that life is out of balance is heard in these statements:

> *During my good times, I'm a workaholic. This is to overcompensate for the times that I just don't think I'm as productive as I should be.*
>
> *I'm an overachiever during my good times to make up for lost time.*

You may feel guilty about past work behavior, so you have difficulty limiting your workload when you are feeling good again. This can lead to a workaholic syndrome during the good times. But more important (and more debilitating), it can lead to feelings of frustration and self-denigration that take the form of:

> *I never complete what I start.*
>
> *I never start those projects that will get me promoted.*

During your good time, look at work patterns that you may have developed to compensate for PMS. Examine both the PMS and non-PMS times. If you are overloading yourself during your good time, you are continuing a pattern that may have developed as a result of PMS. This pattern needs to be changed, and both PMS and non-PMS times might need to be revamped.

Overworking to the point of exhaustion doesn't benefit anyone—not you, your company or your family. Try to even out the workload. It may seem like a good idea to get ahead and do the extras when you are feeling good. But it's more important to budget your energy wisely. A few extras are OK, but too many defeat your purpose.

New Limits on Your Career?

When PMS symptoms accumulate and compound, you can end up on a mental treadmill asking yourself if you are getting too old to accomplish the same amount of work you did when you were younger. You might sense that you can't handle the same stress and tension, and wonder about this because "I'm only 35 years old."

You may feel little continuity in your life. As a result, you may distance yourself psychologically from your work and care less and less about how you do. Your desire to excel may fade, and your main task may become maintenance—coping with the minimum.

What is most likely happening when you psychologically separate from your work is that you also become distanced from your expectations about yourself. You may conclude that you lack merit and are undeserving of any rewards. As Jane, 36, a court stenographer, said:

> *I no longer see myself as worthy or capable of promotions. I sometimes wonder what happened to my career plans.*

Self-Help Exercise

BECOME AWARE OF YOUR WORK PATTERNS

Take a few minutes to think about your typical patterns of work. Now describe them. You might answer questions such as: When do you bring work home? Do you bring too much work home to accomplish? When do you tend to stay after work hours to catch up on your work? What happens when you come home from work? What kind of mood are you usually in? How do you interact with others? What needs to be changed?

Daily ____

____

____

____

Weekly ____

____

____

____

Monthly ____

____

____

____

You can begin to see yourself limited in ways that you never dreamed would limit you. Doors on the horizon that once meant new opportunities now seem closed. And you may not feel like opening any new doors because you are thinking: "I know I can't deal with what's on the other side." You may feel both besieged and cast adrift—as though the world will neither leave you alone nor offer you any opportunities. In short, you can become alienated from your work and from the dreams of a career that once seemed so crucial to your self-fulfillment.

Seeing yourself limited in ways that you are not is a natural side effect of PMS. To see yourself as limited in what you can accomplish or immobilized in your career may have become a way of thinking during your PMS time. This type of thinking can carry over to non-PMS times, and you might stop looking at future possibilities. This can happen easily. Start immediately to tell yourself that this is one of the results of PMS. You can and must see this for what it is. PMS may have been controlling you. Now you are learning how to control it.

Take Reasonable Risks

This way of thinking can develop as a result of PMS, but it doesn't need to continue. Once you have identified the pattern of PMS, you can turn it around to work for you and not against you. Understanding how easily the pattern can develop is only half the job. Now you need to see that again you have the opportunity to take control. For example, if you are a teacher's aide, but you have always wanted to be a teacher, take advantage of your new-found sense of motivation to investigate what is involved in becoming a teacher. Get active! Gather information and share the career idea with a friend or family member who can reinforce your motivation.

Take reasonable risks. With the positive attitude that you are developing, new things are possible. However, don't go overboard. Deciding to become a physician at age 40 may be unrealistic. Make sure the new direction you choose is realistic. By setting achievable goals, even if they are small, you can rebuild a foundation of self-confidence. When you see yourself successfully accomplishing a reasonable goal, you will be inclined to continue building—and building and building.

Take a Positive Approach

Don't become a "workaholic" during your good times to make up for your bad times. This will only make you tired and stressed all the time! Set aside time for exercise, relaxation and social get-togethers throughout the month. Try to stick to your plan. You will be most productive when you approach work refreshed.

Once Again, the Sky's the Limit

I'd like to tell you about a client named Linda whom I counseled at the PMS Clinic. Linda started her career with a major corporation 14 years ago. Over the years, she was promoted steadily until she reached a managerial level. Eventually, however, she was passed over for a big promotion. This left her devastated. She went to her executive director and asked "Why?" The director told her she hadn't been promoted because there was a lot of friction in the department she was managing. It wasn't running smoothly.

Linda's world seemed to be crumbling, as things at home were deteriorating too. She wasn't getting along with her oldest daughter. It seemed that she wasn't managing things at home any better than at work. Her husband suggested she take some time off and get away, but she was too distraught to do this. It seemed ludicrous to her to take time off for a vacation when she was being passed up for promotions. So she began working more diligently at her job.

A couple of months later, she read an article in the *Wall Street Journal*[21] that discussed women in business who had been significantly affected by PMS. Various women with high positions in the business world talked about PMS and its limiting effect on their careers. Linda began to analyze her own situation and realized that most of the confrontations with her workers had occurred during her premenstrual periods. She suspected she had PMS, so she decided to take action and get help.

Four months later, she felt like she was back in charge. From this vantage point, it was clear that PMS symptoms had kept her from being effective in her position. She also realized that if she wanted to advance, she would have to change some of the patterns that had been established with her assistants. She felt competent to do this. In fact, she established a dynamic and successful program for bringing her department together. Six months later, she was once again being considered for promotion.

GETTING A HANDLE ON THE PROBLEM

It is your responsibility to take care of your well-being, including your health and professional reputation. It would be preferable if employers were more understanding regarding PMS, but this is slow in coming. Thus it might be more difficult for you to get understanding and support than it is for an employee who suffers from alcoholism, for example. This is reality, however, so it is up to you to take charge of yourself. Use the following checkpoints to guide you.

✔ *Plan Ahead*

By charting, you can know ahead of time when you will be premenstrual. This means that you can plan ahead and make sure that important engagements are scheduled for a time when you are best able to handle them. If you know that you are going to have a tough assignment, prepare ahead as much as possible.

✔ *Reduce Stress*

Reduce stress in any way possible—especially by taking good care of yourself. For example, at lunchtime, plan to get away and go for a short walk. Better yet, plan to exercise during lunchtime. If this is not possible, plan to exercise as soon as you get home from work.

Additionally, make sure that your diet is as healthy as possible all month long. Follow the diet suggestions outlined in the next chapter. If you try to stay on the diet and develop good eating habits during your good times, it will be easier to stick with them during difficult days. If you do indulge in something salty or sweet, don't degrade yourself—this is one of the most negative patterns that we can develop in having PMS.

Also, get more sleep so that one day's stress and tension does not overflow into the next.

✔ *Talk to Your Employer*

If you are like other PMS sufferers, you might be afraid to bring up the issue of PMS with your employer. This can present a dilemma. Vicki, 34, explained it this way:

> *I want to talk with someone at work, but it's so difficult. I get real nervous. I wonder what they are thinking about me. I get even more nervous when I think I really should say something and then I don't.*

You want and need the understanding and support of your employer, but you may fear that asking for support will be used against you, and you could lose your job.

Because PMS does not yet have the credibility or public recognition as a workplace issue (as do other medical disorders), it usually is not included in employee-assistance programs. It might therefore lack credibility as a factor for failing to work up to par. (This is a good reason to suggest making literature available through the employee-assistance program or in the nurse's office.) It is, nevertheless, better for you to try to find someone who can be supportive than to try to handle the situation alone.

The appropriate person for you to speak with might not be the employer, or even a representative of the employee-assistance program, but rather a friendly co-worker who can bring up the issue to your employer when the time is appropriate.

If you are feeling anxious and guilty about incidents at work, deal with these straightforwardly and take care of them. Don't hold your breath and hope that everyone will forget that anything ever happened. It is important for you to address the issue so you can alleviate the guilt and anxiety you have built up.

It might be especially difficult for you to talk convincingly about your situation if you must first legitimize it in your own mind. Therefore, talk to your employer when you are feeling self-confident and assertive. Present your situation as a matter of fact. You can tell your boss or supervisor that:

- You are dealing with a physically-based medical disorder that requires treatment.
- You are working hard to get it resolved.
- You expect it to be taken care of within the foreseeable future.

It is not necessary for you to name PMS. Taking care of yourself does not require that you feed other people's stereotypical thinking. Neither is it necessary for you to apologize. You may not get the response you want, but understanding is more likely if the issue is discussed than if it is not.

As important as it is to talk with your boss, however, in a few cases this may not be helpful. Only you can decide if this is the case for you. The most important goal is to relieve your symptoms, not add to them. If talking with your employer will increase your stress rather than decrease it, then concentrate instead on your own treatment program. The last thing you need if you suffer from PMS is extra tension. With time, your efforts will have a positive effect at work.

IF YOU ARE AN EMPLOYER

Industries are slowly but surely realizing that most of their employees' personal problems have a significant effect on work, productivity and profits. Many progressive companies with employee-assistance programs already understand the value of supporting their workers. They are making available to their employees brochures and referral services for PMS. Their progressive stance will hopefully extend to other industries. This would make it acceptable for a woman to acknowledge that she sometimes needs assistance with PMS, with both the individual woman and the employer realizing the payoff.

Education at the Workplace

Education regarding PMS is an important workplace issue that deserves the same attention as alcoholism. Most employers already understand the negative effect of alcoholism on productivity, and it can be used as the framework of discussion about PMS in order to get assistance for employees who suffer from it.

The woman with PMS should be able to ask for help without having to embarrass herself or jeopardize her job. The employer's perspective should, ideally, be the same as it is towards alcoholism in the workplace: "Let's get some treatment."

Perhaps more important is the need for mutual employer/employee understanding about PMS. The woman who suffers from PMS needs to know that there is some understanding on the part of the employer. This is especially true if she makes an effort to be open about her problem. She should have an avenue to discuss the problem *before* she is ready to quit or have a nervous breakdown.

Education at the workplace is a must if conditions are to change. Employers would be wise to pay attention to an area that affects production and profits, while not forgetting the cost to employees of stress and discomfort.

CHAPTER 9

GETTING BETTER:

Taking Care of All of You

MAUREEN'S STORY

I've been through every stage of PMS that you can think of—from start to finish! I no longer suffer from it, and my life is finally happy and together.

About 7 years ago, things started going wrong. I became extremely restless and unhappy with my life. I got divorced, quit one career and started another. But it seemed that I was becoming less—not more—content. It took me quite a while to find out that my problem might be PMS. When I did find out, I jumped at the opportunity to learn as much as possible because I didn't like the person I was becoming. I was tremendously relieved to find out that I was not *going through some incurable depression, but that I had something treatable.*

I heard about PMS from a friend who belonged to a PMS support group. She invited me to join. What a find! What was most important about this group was the understanding and empathy that I felt from other women. Looking back on it now, I can see that this was crucial. I started exercising a couple of times a week with one of the other women in the support group. We'd go hiking in the hills in the early morning. These moments soon became the highlight of the day. After a couple of months, we were hiking every morning. We were hooked!

While we hiked, we'd share new bits of information about PMS. We talked about our daily struggles and victories over junk food. Coffee was my crutch—her weakness was salty food. We got to the point where we looked forward to telling each other something like, "I only

> *ate a handful of potato chips today."*
>
> *The more we exercised and talked about changing our eating patterns, the easier it was to do. Then a subtle shift occurred. We talked less and less of feelings of deprivation—"giving up this or that"—and more and more about the healthy foods we* could *eat. We shared recipes that we had successfully prepared. We got to where we enjoyed eating as nutritiously as possible and exercising as much as possible because we wanted to feel as good as possible.*
>
> *I can honestly say I haven't felt this good about myself or been in such good physical shape since I was in my teens.*

JOIN A SUPPORT GROUP

Every health problem involves mind and body. With PMS, we feel our psychological and emotional symptoms strongest, so it is logical to take care of our emotions first. For this reason, I strongly urge you to call on your women friends for support. Don't isolate yourself, don't withdraw.

Create a supportive and sharing environment with other women. Join a support group. It is very important to have your feelings validated. The best way to do this is to share your emotional and psychological experiences with other women who understand what you are going through. In the process, you are also validating their perceptions, emotions and thoughts.

We are usually intuitively aware that the source of our symptoms is physical. Unfortunately, we have learned to distrust our intuition. Relearning that trust is a goal of treatment. If you join a support group, you will find validation for your intuitions and feelings. This is a crucial aspect of getting better.

It's always a good idea to express what's going on in our minds. It's an especially good idea when you are suffering from PMS. By joining a support group, you can gain an understanding that you are not alone. You will also learn from other women about the subtleties and nuances of PMS. Their understanding can see you through your feelings of isolation, and they can support you in changing your exercise and eating habits. You can learn to identify and acknowledge your strengths and accomplishments, even if they are small.

When considering treatment for PMS, it makes sense to start with diet, vitamins and exercise. If these do not prove effective in alleviating symptoms of PMS, then—and only then—should prescription medications be considered.

Every expert in the field has a slightly different idea about what constitutes the best approach to treating PMS. Keep in mind that there is no one right diet, exercise and vitamin program. Our goal will be to find the treatment plan that suits you best.

In this chapter, we are are first going to look at some common approaches to (mis)treating PMS—quick fixes that don't work. Then we will explore the most current information available on diet, vitamins, exercise and progesterone therapy. I do not explore other drug therapies because not enough is known about them, and research about them is inconclusive.

QUICK FIXES THAT DON'T WORK

Since PMS has been identified, there have been several over-the-counter preparations that claim to alleviate symptoms of PMS. Most of these contain a mild antihistamine, a mild diuretic and an analgesic. However, there haven't been any studies that prove these are effective for PMS symptoms.

Diuretics and Tranquilizers

Have you ever been to a doctor for PMS symptoms and been told there's really nothing wrong with you, only to be handed a prescription for a tranquilizer and a diuretic? This should raise some questions in your mind because the tranquilizer suggests that you have a problem in your head and the diuretic suggests that you have a problem in your body!

Diuretics are prescribed based upon this rationale: if you are retaining fluid in your breasts, your abdomen, your fingers and toes, you might also be retaining fluid in your brain tissue, making nerve endings more irritable.

Diuretics may relieve bloating and breast soreness, but they are fairly ineffective in treating PMS symptoms such as irritability and depression. Some diuretics can throw your body chemistry off-balance by depleting your body's supply of potassium. If enough potassium is lost, an electrolyte imbalance can result, leading to heavy

Take a Positive Approach

Having PMS presents an opportunity for growth. This may sound strange, but it is a good way to approach the problem. Once you recognize that PMS is a medical disorder, you have more motivation to examine your eating and exercise habits. Approach the treatment of PMS as a good way of getting your life in order.

perspiration, weakness and light-headedness. One client described getting out of bed in the morning, stretching, and feeling so weak that she fell back into bed! If you are looking for a way to decrease fluid retention, consider cutting down on your salt intake. Some doctors also recommend drinking unsweetened grapefruit juice as a natural diuretic.

Anti-depressants and tranquilizers are commonly prescribed for PMS symptoms. Valium® (diazepam by generic name) seems to be one of the most popular and it is often prescribed over long periods of time. Many women understandably worry about using tranquilizers over a long period of time. Some tranquilizers are habit-forming, and carry risks associated with long-term use. While anti-depressants are generally not habit-forming, both anti-depressants and tranquilizers can cause adverse reactions and side effects.

Hysterectomies

Doctors sometimes recommend hysterectomies to deal with PMS symptoms. The reason seems to be: "If it bothers you, take it out!" You can, of course, have pathological problems that indicate the need for a hysterectomy. But if you have a hysterectomy for PMS symptoms in the absence of pathological problems, you are simply buying yourself time.

This is what I mean. Many women whom I have counseled report that after a hysterectomy, their PMS symptoms subsided or disappeared temporarily, only to reappear several months later. They often ask, "How can I have these symptoms if I no longer have menstrual periods?" The answer is that most hysterectomies are partial hysterectomies. The ovaries are left in the woman's body and the uterus is taken out. The woman's body cycles hormonally as it did before the hysterectomy, so it is easy to see how PMS symptoms can return following surgery.

The first month that the symptoms reappear, a woman thinks, "It must be the kids," or "The weather's been lousy," or she finds some other reason for feeling so low. When the symptoms go away, she stops thinking about it. But when the symptoms return the next month, she panics. Despite the hysterectomy, she can identify the exact day that her period would have started. How does she know? Her symptoms are reappearing again on schedule, and they are back in full force.

She might start experiencing depression, irritability, lethargy—all symptoms of PMS. Most likely she will call her physician and say:

> *You know a year ago when I had that hysterectomy? Well, I feel even worse now.*

In response, the doctor might tell her that she needs to see a therapist. A common response is that it couldn't have anything to do with her reproductive system because that problem has already been dealt with.

The Pill

Doctors prescribe oral contraceptives for a variety of reasons, including attempts to treat PMS. However, a significant number of women who have PMS do not tolerate birth-control pills very well. If you have PMS and you are taking oral contraceptives, your PMS symptoms can be exacerbated. As Eileen, 27, who works as a waitress, said:

> *I just couldn't take the pill. I had to get off it. The symptoms that I had when I was on the pill were too severe.*

Oral contraceptives frequently contain synthetic progesterone (progest*ogen*). Synthetic progestogens can intensify symptoms of PMS because when they are present in your body, they suppress your body's production of progesterone. Your body perceives synthetic progest*ogens* as progesterone, and reduces its already-deficient progesterone output.

Women who have migraine headaches seem particularly susceptible to these changes. One research study found that migraines did not begin for some women until they began taking birth-control pills. In other women who had previously experienced migraines, headaches intensified after they began taking birth-control pills.[22]

A Final Word of Warning

The "quick fixes" discussed here not only fail in treating PMS, they may make the situation worse. Some birth-control pills intensify PMS, hysterectomies do not cure PMS, and tranquilizers and anti-depressants only mask PMS symptoms. Tranquilizers especially have the potential for being abused. Think of the addictive pattern that could develop if a woman used tranquilizers on a regular basis. Think also of the danger in having large doses of tranquilizers available to a woman who feels suicidal.

Before considering using *any* medication, you should undertake self-help measures to see what changes they can bring about. If your symptoms are not significantly relieved after trying these methods, you should consider consulting a clinic or physician well-educated in PMS for further medical treatment.

FOOD FOR THOUGHT

Fresh fruit, grains, vegetables, legumes, nuts and cereals make up our nutritional heritage—the foods that historically shaped the physiological development of our bodies. These foods are rich in complex carbohydrates, vitamins and minerals that convert food into energy in a way that is optimal for our bodies. Today's typical diet deviates from this natural diet, however, and includes red meat, refined sugar and processed foods.

It is important to eat the healthiest foods possible throughout your cycle, but it is especially important during the time between ovulation and menstruation. During this time, your biochemistry is altered due to hormonal change. Blood-sugar is more unstable. To prevent erratic changes in your body's chemistry, you need to keep your body's blood sugar on an even level. Therefore, your first line of treatment for PMS should be dietary.

What is Blood Sugar?

Glucose (blood sugar) is the basic fuel that runs your body. Nearly all tissues in the body depend on it to function. The brain and nervous system are especially affected by it. Your body has mechanisms to stabilize and store blood sugar and keep it within normal limits. When blood sugar is too low, symptoms such as irritability, panic, angry outbursts, migraine headaches and weakened muscles develop.

Your blood-sugar level fluctuates in relationship to your food intake and your physical and mental activity. When you eat, your blood-sugar level rises, and your pancreas secretes insulin to keep it from going too high. When you engage in activity, you use the sugar stored in the blood. When glucose levels are reduced, the body can convert fat and protein to make new sugar, as well as release stored sugar into the bloodstream.

During PMS times we crave foods that provide quick energy—foods that will raise the blood sugar to a high level. But these foods usually contain refined sugar, and thus raise your blood sugar too high. The problem is that later there will be a corresponding drop in blood sugar as your body responds to the high level. A "high high" produces a corresponding "low low." This can make you feel as if you're taking a roller-coaster ride, both in terms of your energy and your emotions.

Complex carbohydrates, those with a complex structure of starches and fiber, help stabilize blood sugar. Complex carbohydrates include whole grains, such as wheat, barley, corn, oats, brown rice, rye, millet, buckwheat and fresh vegetables. Because these foods have a complex structure, they break down slowly, are digested slowly, and release sugar into the system slowly. This stabilizes blood sugar and causes it to rise slowly, peak slowly and fall slowly. When your blood sugar is stabilized, so are your moods, your energy and your desire to eat.

To keep your blood sugar on an even level, follow these suggestions:

✔ *Eat Often*

Going for long periods of time without eating disrupts the blood-sugar process. If you feel bloated due to water retention—a very common symptom of PMS—you may think you should quit eating for a while, or even go on a strict diet. If you go a long interval without food, however, your blood sugar drops to a very low level. This sets the stage for an angry outburst, a migraine headache or an anxiety attack.

This cycle can be prevented if you learn to eat as you did when you were young. Observe how toddlers eat. When they get up in the morning, they are usually very hungry for breakfast, and by midmorning they want a snack. At lunch, they settle for half of a sandwich. By midafternoon, they are ready for another snack, and at dinnertime, they eat a moderate-sized dinner.

Compare this to the way adults tend to eat. Often, we skip breakfast and sometimes lunch, and then have a ridiculously large dinner. Even if you didn't have PMS, eating in this fashion would be unhealthy.

If you do have PMS, it is imperative to start eating more frequently and more nutritiously so that you can begin to gain a sense of control. A general rule of thumb is to never go more than 3 hours during the day without eating—especially if you are carrying out a lot of mental or physical work.

✔ *Avoid Sugar*

If you suffer from PMS, your body is probably less tolerant of refined sugar. Refined sugar can trigger and intensify your PMS symptoms of fatigue, headaches, anxiety, dizziness and irritability. These symptoms are similar to the symptoms of hypoglycemia (low blood sugar caused by abnormal function of the pancreas). Additionally, sugar depletes the body's B-complex vitamins and minerals, which can also exacerbate PMS symptoms.

The preferred treatment for both PMS and hypoglycemia—the one that most physicians recommend—is diet management. If you have PMS, you should follow a hypoglycemic diet throughout the month (not only during the time when you are premenstrual). This diet consists of 5 or 6 small meals a day that include protein and complex carbohydrates, but are low in simple carbohydrates (sugar) and moderate in fats. Until you do this, you will not be fully treating your symptoms. Your body becomes conditioned to react to food in a particular way. The idea is to train your body to use food optimally all month long.

Changing Your Diet

Everyone agrees that the first line of treatment for PMS should be dietary. Keep in mind that dietary habits are some of the most difficult—but not impossible—to change. Remember, nobody says it's going to be easy for you, but it's worth it!

The best strategy is to first become aware of your eating habits. You can accomplish this through charting. Then you need to begin to make necessary diet changes. These should also be charted. It is optimal to have a healthy diet during the entire month, but especially important when you are premenstrual.

Your diet should be low in caffeine, salt, sugar, and alcohol (all the things we want) and it should emphasize fresh fruits, vegetables and other forms of complex carbohydrates. It is especially important to reduce refined sugar and salts, and increase complex carbohydrates.

If you're feeling tired and lethargic, high-potassium foods such as bananas, broccoli, tomatoes, cantaloupe and potatoes are helpful. Avocados, fish, poultry and whole grains are foods rich in vitamin B6, the vitamin that affects certain mood-regulating brain chemicals. Finally, there are many benefits to reducing your salt intake. Your bloating, swelling and weight gain may dwindle in significance and intensity. High blood pressure may also be lowered by reducing the amount of salt you eat.

Diet Changes

Increase intake of	**Decrease intake of**
Fish	Sugar
Poultry	Salt, high-sodium foods
Whole grains	Highly processed foods
Legumes	Red meats
Fresh fruits	Caffeine
Vegetables	Alcohol
Safflower, sesame, sunflower oils	Chocolate
Water	Fatty foods
	Nicotine

VITAMINS

It has been well-documented that a woman's biochemistry changes when she is premenstrual. It is a very good idea to supplement your diet (even if it is a well-balanced diet) with a vitamin and mineral supplement. One that has been developed particularly for PMS symptoms can be ordered through Madison Pharmacy Associates, through PMS Access (see address on page 169). PMS Access is a great source of information to find out what works best for you. They will discuss the options with you as to what the best vitamin program for you should be.

Vitamin Needs

Vitamin	Suggested Daily Supplement	Function	Food Source
A	15,000 I.U.	Alleviates premenstrual acne and oily skin.	Carrots, apricots, turnip greens, salmon, squash, dandelion greens, sweet red peppers.
B Complex (riboflavin, niacin, thiamin)	50mg to 100mg	Prevents loss of the B vitamins caused by emotional stress, which results in irritability and fatigue.	Whole grains, liver and legumes.
B_6	Doses from 50mg to 200mg*	Minimizes many premenstrual symptoms such as food cravings, fluid retention, irritability, breast tenderness, fatigue and mood swings. Has been linked to release of the brain's neurotransmitters, dopamine and serotonin, which elevate mood. Plays a part in the metabolism of carbohydrates and proteins and can reduce food cravings when taken premenstrually.	Chicken, shrimp, tuna, salmon, wheat grains, soybeans, peas, beans, yeast.
E	300 I.U. to 600 I.U.	Helps to reduce fibrocystic disease (benign lumps in the breasts).	Broccoli, asparagus, whole grains, wheat germ, turnip greens, sweet potatoes, safflower oil.

Vitamin Needs (continued)

Calcium	150mg	Helps prevent menstrual cramps.	Salmon, shrimp, soybeans, tofu, sesame seeds, carob, collard leaves, blackstrap molasses.
Magnesium	300mg	Helps prevent menstrual cramps, helps control sugar cravings.	Salmon, shrimp, tofu, lima beans, red beans, black-eyed peas, whole wheat and rye breads.
Zinc	25mg	Helps control acne.	Wheat, chicken, rice bran, black-eyed peas, buckwheat, corn, onions, apples, cabbage, berries.
C	250mg to 1,000mg	Helps control stress and premenstrual allergies.	Citrus fruits, berries, cabbage, sweet red peppers, strawberries, cauliflower.
D	100 I.U. (should not be taken in large doses)	Helps control premenstrual acne.	Exposure to sunlight or supplements added to foods, primarily dairy products.

*For PMS, do not take vitamin B_6 by itself. Rather, the entire complex of B vitamins should be taken together. The recommended daily doses of B_6 and B-complex are: 100mg of B complex and 50-200mg of B_6. When you are premenstrual, increase the B_6 dosage to 200mg to 500mg. To maximize absorption and avoid stomach irritation, the B vitamins should be taken with meals.

Unless you are well-educated about vitamins, consult a doctor or nutritionist before taking non-prescription vitamins for PMS. If you choose to take a combination of vitamins that you put together, make sure that your diet includes the vitamins and minerals listed above.

FOOD CRAVINGS

Food cravings can be a big problem for many women who suffer from PMS. They can relate to the self-esteem issues of PMS. As Anne, an education consultant, explained:

> *I stick to my diet during my good times, but during my bad times I'm dreadful. I eat everything that doesn't move faster than I do! Then, of course, I hate myself and think that I'm fat. This makes me think that no diet can help me, and I begin to binge on chocolates and salty foods. I hate myself, but do I stop eating? No!*

Food cravings can present a psychological dilemma. They can set off a cycle that is especially harmful to your body when you are premenstrual. The cycle works like this: you eat uncontrollably, then condemn yourself for it, swear to stick to your diet, and begin to fast again. Because you feel guilty about overeating, your self-esteem is lowered and you become depressed. You may even entertain the idea that you have an eating disorder.

If you have food cravings and you know that they are associated with PMS, you probably wonder why you can't control them. Premenstrual food cravings are physical—they result from changes in blood-sugar levels, or they result from a mineral deficiency in your body. However great your self-control, you cannot suppress these cravings through willpower. Often dieting can trigger a food craving because it causes your blood-sugar level to fall significantly.

If you crave chocolate when you are premenstrual, it can be a sign of magnesium deficiency. Chocolate is high in magnesium, and this mineral is deficient in many women during their PMS time. Fight your chocolate cravings by replacing the chocolate with complex carbohydrates. Additionally, consider taking a vitamin that supplements the magnesium in your diet.

If you have food cravings, first determine if they are PMS-related. Chart them

Take a Positive Approach

Your eating habits probably affect everyone in your family. When you cut back on your own sugar and salt intake, you are setting a good example for your children. You are showing them how to cultivate good dietary habits that can stay with them for the rest of their lives.

along with your other symptoms to determine if they occur in a pattern. Then make the necessary dietary changes to prevent these cravings. If you follow the following suggestions, you should have success.

✔ *Take Control Over What You Eat*

Plan your menus for each day. Plan your snacks too. It is admirable to decide that you will eat more healthfully, but if your approach is not a planned and reasonable one, your best intentions are likely to fall short.

✔ *Avoid "Instant Cures"*

You might want to start a new eating regimen for yourself right away—a diet that eliminates a lot of the foods that you have been used to eating. You might decide: "I'm going to make all of the necessary changes right now, and I'm going to be perfect in sticking to my diet." Beware! This is a scenario for failure. Try to avoid it. It is preferable to come up with a diet in which you plan to make changes that are both *reasonable* and *gradual*. If you work outside the home, remember that healthy dietary changes need to be *practical* as well.

✔ *Plan Ahead*

Determine when your low-energy times occur (for many people, this is late afternoon) and have a snack ready. If you do not have a healthy snack on hand when you are at work, chances are you will eat the junk food that's in the vending machine down the hall. To make it easier, shop and have separate groceries that you don't unpack at home. Take them to work at the beginning of the week and keep them there so they are available for you. You can also fix fresh fruits and vegetables each night to take to work the next day.

✔ *Give Yourself Credit for Trying*

Do not expect perfection. Do not unduly criticize yourself if you do not follow your diet perfectly. If you have already eaten five candy bars, don't punish yourself. Simply tell yourself: "I ate too much sugar, I know it's not a good idea, and I'll make sure that in the future I have plenty of fresh fruit on hand so I won't be tempted to do it again."

Remember that the idea of the diet is to make you feel better, not worse. As you gain more and more control over your eating habits and your PMS, you will see the benefits and reap the rewards. In the meantime, give yourself credit for the changes that you have made.

✔ *Make Changes During Your Good Time*

You need to change your diet when you are most motivated and most likely to stick

Diet Problems and Solutions

Item	Problem	Solution
Animal protein, especially beef and poultry.	Synthetic estrogens are injected into some cattle and poultry. Eating too much protein increases your body's need for some minerals.	Substitute other sources of protein, especially fish and vegetable proteins such as whole grains, seeds, nuts, beans and peas. Eat no more than three 3-oz. servings of protein a day.
Salt (and high-sodium foods)	Worsens fluid retention, bloating and breast tenderness.	Substitute postassium-based salt substitutes. Use herbs, lemon juice and vinegar to flavor foods.
Sugar	Causes blood sugar to fluctuate too much. Depletes the body's B-complex vitamins and minerals.	Avoid artificial sweeteners and refined sugar. If you do eat sweets, eat them with well-balanced meals to slow sugar metabolism.
Alcohol	Interferes with formation of glucose, prolonging low blood sugar and intensifying irritability, anxiety, headaches and dizziness. Disrupts the liver's ability to metabolize hormones, causing higher-than-normal estrogen.	Substitute light wine and beer, or non-alcoholic drinks such as mineral water with a twist of lime.
Chocolate	Increases craving for sugar and caffeine. Causes breast tenderness. Increases demand for B-complex vitamins.	Substitute carob. Eat foods high in magnesium (shrimp, salmon, whole grains, beans and peas).
Caffeine	Causes fibrocystic breast disease. Causes breast tenderness.	Substitute fruit juices, decaffeinated coffee and tea, and herbal teas.

with the changes. It is unlikely that you will be able to change your eating habits during your PMS time and stick to them. Set up the pattern when you are strongest.

✔ *Establish Good Eating Habits All Month Long*

Eat as nutritiously as you can. You deserve the best all the time, so eat only the best foods (which are not, by any means, the most expensive foods). Eating the best foods all the time trains your body to be more balanced and energetic and keeps your emotions even.

Self-Help Exercise

PLAN YOUR MEALS

Controlling what you eat is much easier if you have a clear plan. Think about what you want to eat today. Then take a minute to write it down. This will make it more "do-able" for you.

Breakfast ______________________________

____

____

Snack ______________________________

Lunch ______________________________

____

____

Snack ______________________________

Dinner ______________________________

____

____

Snack ______________________________

CAFFEINE

Caffeine, which is found in coffee, tea and cola, can cause breast tenderness and exacerbate fibrocystic breast disease (benign lumps in a woman's breasts). Caffeine also increases mood swings, irritability and anxiety. It depletes vitamin B in the body, and it interferes with the metabolism of carbohydrates.

Caffeine is one of those substances that causes blood sugar to rise. When the effect wears off, blood sugar drops dramatically. The goal is to stabilize blood sugar, so caffeine needs to be avoided.

This may not be as easy as it sounds. If you have used caffeine for a long time to energize yourself, you may have developed a dependency on it. If so, you might not be able to quit caffeine abruptly because this can cause caffeine-withdrawal headaches.

If you have been drinking coffee, tea or colas throughout the day, you have probably been using them for more than just caffeine boosts. Most likely, you are also getting a break from your work routine by sitting down with a cup of coffee, a glass of tea or a can of cola. The beverage has provided more than caffeine for you—it has provided time out for a break.

One way to reduce caffeine consumption is to stop all at once. But it's preferable to try a more reasonable and workable approach. If you are drinking more than four or five cups of coffee a day, cut down gradually. Cut your caffeine consumption in half the first week by brewing your coffee with half caffeine and half water-processed decaffeinated coffee. This way, you can have the customary four to five cups of coffee a day, but you are getting only half the caffeine. The next week, cut your caffeine consumption in half again and brew your coffee with a 3:1 ratio of decaffeinated coffee to regular coffee. Continue to reduce caffeine this way until you are no longer using caffeine. You still will be having your four or five cups of coffee—decaffeinated. Perhaps most important, you will still be getting your time-outs.

Take a Positive Approach

A coffee break is more than a beverage break—it is a social occasion. Don't cut out coffee breaks because you are reducing your caffeine intake. When you're invited for a cup of coffee, accept the invitation. But remember to bring your own decaffeinated coffee or tea, or juice.

ALCOHOL

PMS can cause you to question your sanity on a monthly basis, and your self-esteem also suffers regular blows. The resulting anxieties and pressures can tempt you to use alcohol or other drugs to get you through your PMS time of the month. The relief is temporary, however. Use of drugs tends to compound, not alleviate, the problem.

When you are premenstrual and drink alcohol, you are doing so at the very time when your body is least able to tolerate alcohol. Alcohol disrupts your liver's ability to metabolize certain hormones and to form new glucose. This is compounded by the change in your biochemistry when you are premenstrual. Your altered tolerance to alcohol makes you feel the effects of one or two drinks as if they were three or four. Your ability to think clearly and effectively will also be disproportionately impaired. Alcohol is a depressant, so it compounds the mental-physical depression of PMS.

According to information gathered at the PMS Clinic, use of alcohol and other drugs is dramatically increased during the premenstrual phase. Of the women who drink alcohol when they are premenstrual, 57% report exaggerated effects of alcohol during the premenstrual phase, while 70% report an increased desire for alcohol at that time. As Barb, 37, a marketing agent, said:

> *Yes, I do use alcohol and cigarettes to get through the toughest times. Why shouldn't I? I need something to help me deal with the anxiety.*

The physical intolerance for alcohol when you are premenstrual makes you very vulnerable to alcoholic cycles. The resulting pattern of drinking can be detrimental to your self-image and self-esteem. For example, because you cannot cope very well at work, you might leave work and have a drink to relieve the pressure and anxiety that have built up over the day. One drink leads to another, however, and the next day, you can be less able to cope with work than the day before. Ultimately, you might drink to escape the consequences of drinking itself.

The medical and mental-health professions need to be more sensitive to the possible relationship between PMS and alcohol intolerance.

EXERCISE

Exercise is one of the most important ways to control PMS. Why? Because exerting yourself physically gives your body an opportunity to release pent-up tension and anxiety. As a result of exercising, your brain produces endorphins that relieve pain and elevate your mood. Exercise thus brings on a feeling of physical health and emotional well-being. A good workout makes you feel at peace with yourself. Perhaps most important, exercise helps you like yourself. By exercising, you know that you are doing something that is really good for you.

Think of exercise as a preventive measure. You are giving your body and your mind a chance to release pressure and tension before it builds up. By exercising and releasing tension—both psychological and physical—you are also providing yourself an opportunity to relax. This helps prevent an angry outburst when you are premenstrual.

Contrary to everything that you probably learned when you were growing up, moderate exercise does not wear you out. Lack of exercise depresses the body, not the other way around. Exercise energizes and relaxes you.

Many experts recommend exercising on a daily basis. Obviously, this isn't always possible. Try to make this a future goal rather than a new regimen that must be put into effect tomorrow morning! For tomorrow, next week, and the next several months, set up an exercise routine that suits you and is within your reach. Avoid any plan that sets you up for failure. Do not promise yourself that you will exercise every day, for example, if you have never been successful at this before.

Be *practical* and *reasonable* about what you can and cannot do. For now, I suggest setting aside 30 to 45 minutes three times a week. Consider this a minimum. After a month or so, you will probably find that you want to exercise more. Why? Because exercise makes you feel good, so it's easy to get hooked on it.

For PMS, there are many different approaches to exercise. Some experts say it is best to exercise outdoors, some say that yoga and relaxation exercises are the best, and some focus on stress-reduction exercises. All of these are potentially beneficial. You are your own best judge as to what will work for you. A good place to begin is with an exercise that you enjoy. If you like to ride a bike, start with this. On the other hand, if you've never liked swimming, don't decide that now's the time to start swimming. Again, avoid setting yourself up for failure.

Take a Positive Approach

Take an activist approach to the day. The sooner you get moving, the sooner you feel better. Early morning can be the optimal time to exercise when you are premenstrual. By exercising in the morning, you increase your blood circulation first thing and steady your heart rate. You can work out the physical and psychological anxiety that builds up if you have nightmares (a common symptom of PMS). If you are married and have young children, exercising in the morning while the kids are asleep means Daddy is available in case they wake up.

You can reduce depression by becoming active. Of course, when you are most depressed is when it is most difficult to get up and move—so you may need to plan ways to motivate yourself. You might want to ask someone to exercise with you—maybe your husband or boyfriend. Hearing someone else say, "Let's go for a brisk walk" can be more appealing that the thought of exercising by yourself. Or, you might try exercising with your toddler. You might put your toddler in a bike seat in the back of your bike and go for a ride, or exercise to music together, or push your child in a stroller. Exercise is something you can do without separating yourself from your child, and it will benefit both of you.

Another approach is to get away and exercise—away from the stresses of your everyday life. Getting in the car and driving to an exercise spa can be a way to take time out for yourself and get some exercise at the same time. After exercising, take a long shower and have a leisurely walk or drive home. The break will do you good, not to mention the exercise. This way, exercise will be something that you look forward to instead of being a dreaded chore.

Get started when you feel good. Unfortunately, when we are in the middle of PMS, we are not likely to be motivated to start an exercise program. If you start the exercise routine when you are not premenstrual, your motivation will be at its highest. Then chances of continuing your exercise program during your PMS time are much better.

PROGESTERONE THERAPY

Progesterone therapy is supplementation of the body's supply of progesterone. Progesterone is one of the two principal female hormones, and the body produces it during the second half of the menstrual cycle (starting at ovulation) as well as during pregnancy. One of the most commonly held theories about the origin of PMS is that a woman suffers from PMS because her body does not produce sufficient levels of progesterone during the premenstrual phase of her cycle. The purpose of progesterone therapy is to raise the body's progesterone level during that time.

Take a Positive Approach

Give yourself permission not to be perfect. Don't punish or criticize yourself when you don't follow your exercise program exactly. As you gain more control over PMS, you will see the benefits and reap the rewards. In the meantime, be firm—but gentle—with yourself.

Use of progesterone in clinical practice indicates that it can be effective in the treatment of severe symptoms associated with PMS, although it has not been shown to help *all* women. However, numerous testimonials from women who have used progesterone therapy suggest that it can relieve severe physical symptoms such as migraine headaches. Women report that progesterone has minimized erratic, self-destructive and dangerous behaviors. These behaviors include angry outbursts that can lead to quitting a job, rage that can result in child abuse, anger and resentment that can lead to divorce, and the kind of desperate depression that can make a woman feel suicidal.

A Few Words of Caution

The use of natural progesterone has been approved by the Federal Drug Administration (FDA) for human use, and it is often prescribed in Europe as a treatment during the early stages of pregnancy in women who have a tendency toward spontaneous abortion. Progesterone has not, however, been approved by the FDA specifically for the treatment of PMS. No drug has been approved by the FDA for the treatment of PMS, although diuretics, tranquilizers, birth-control pills, and anti-depressants are often prescribed for women who suffer from PMS. Because current information indicates that progesterone poses low risks for patients, and because it seems to eliminate severe PMS symptoms, many physicians are now prescribing it for the treatment of PMS.

However, although many women have reported relief from their symptoms with progesterone treatment, this mode of treatment needs to be scientifically validated. There are no studies available yet that adequately examine the possible long-term effects of progesterone.

Women are sometimes concerned about the possible carcinogenic effects of progesterone. It should be noted that Dr. Dalton has been prescribing progesterone for more than 30 years in England. She reports no increase in incidences of cancer among: (1) 120 women who have been on progesterone therapy for 5 years; and (2) 19 women who have been on progesterone therapy for over 15 years.[23] However, the number of women that she has treated and studied is too small to provide conclusive evidence.

Interestingly enough, some research strongly indicates that progesterone deficiency in women increases the risk of cancer. Summarizing this research, Dr. Ronald Norris states: "A recent study in women evaluated for infertility suggested that progesterone deficiency increased the risk of premenopausal breast cancer 5.4 times and increased the risk of death from all malignant neoplasms 10.0 times."[24]

Thus, while there is no definitive scientific statement about the use of progesterone for the treatment of PMS, there are indications—both of a scientific and testimonial nature—that appear favorable.

What is the risk?

Is it better to deal with the symptoms of PMS or risk using a medication that is somewhat experimental but can possibly alleviate the symptoms? Make as informed a decision as possible. If you are considering using progesterone, it is very important that you gather as much information as possible regarding its action and possible side effects. Currently research is being carried out at Vanderbilt University, Duke University and the National Institute of Mental Health (NIMH) to determine the effectiveness and possible side effects of progesterone. An excellent source for information regarding the track record of progesterone is Madison Pharmacy Associates in Madison, Wisconsin. This pharmaceutical company markets progesterone products, and is a nationally recognized organization for consultation about management of PMS. A toll-free number, 800-558-7046, is available for information. This organization publishes a bimonthly newsletter, *PMS Access*, that addresses current developments about PMS. The newsletter is available by subscription, and the address is listed on page 169.

If you are concerned about possible side effects of progesterone, you owe it to yourself to investigate it thoroughly, and update yourself often about new developments in this field. Never use any medication—progesterone or any other medication—until your questions have been answered satisfactorily. If you do, you will be defeating your own purpose. Why? Because, if you are preoccupied with the possible negative effects of a medication, you will be trading one kind of stress for another.

How should you decide about using progesterone?

If you are still suffering from PMS symptoms after trying all the self-help treatments for PMS, you must decide if your symptoms are severe enough that they necessitate progesterone therapy. In making the decision, you need to weigh the risks between possible long-term side effects of progesterone against the consequences of PMS symptoms.

What is the best way for you to go about deciding whether you should use progesterone? If I were counseling you at the PMS Clinic, I would ask you: "Are your symptoms interfering significantly with your personal or professional life?"

If your answer was "yes," then you might benefit from progesterone therapy. If your PMS symptoms are damaging your relationships and your self-esteem, you need to stop the destructive process and stabilize your situation. You need to find a doctor who can assist you in getting effective medical treatment.

How is progesterone administered?

If you are considering using progesterone therapy, you need to consult your physician. However, he or she might not be familiar with progesterone therapy as a treatment for PMS. If this is the case, you might want to refer him or her to the references listed in the resource guide on page 168.

Progesterone usually is not taken orally because it is inactivated by the liver. There are three main methods of administering progesterone:

- Suppositories (rectal and vaginal)
- Liquid suspension (a liquid administered with a rectal syringe)
- Intramuscular injections

Additionally, some doctors are prescribing sublingual (under the tongue) capsules. There are pros and cons to all of these methods. Suppositories are usually more expensive than rectal suspension. Additionally, some women complain that they cause temporary discomfort. Rectal suspension costs less and is reported to be more comfortable to use. Intramuscular injections are more painful and require regular visits to the doctor.

If you choose to use progesterone, it is important for you to become educated about the importance of administering it at the the correct times in the cycle. Two things are important. Progesterone therapy needs to be started *before* symptoms appear, and it needs to be administered on a very regular basis. Skipping times or administering it in an erratic fashion can produce an erratic cycle. This is counterproductive. The goal is to stabilize and balance your body.

Is progesterone a natural or synthetic substance?

Progesterone is a natural substance. Natural progesterone is derived from soybeans and a certain type of yams. (However, *eating* these foods does not increase your progesterone level.) The molecules of these natural substances are slightly changed to produce a chemical duplicate of human progesterone. To alleviate the symptoms of PMS, progesterone must be taken in its natural form.

A word of warning: Synthetic progesterone is of no value in treating PMS. Synthetic progesterone is called progest*ogen* or progest*in*. Chemically it does not duplicate natural progesterone. This is important because physicians often erroneously prescribe progesto*gens* (oral medications) for the treatment of PMS. These synthetic progesto*gens* have an effect on the endometrium (lining of the uterus), but because they are not metabolized by progesterone receptors, they do not affect the brain or other organs.[25]

Dr. Dalton has summarized the reasons why progesto*gens* are not substitutes for progesterone: (1) synthetic progesto*gen* lowers the level of progesterone in the blood; (2) progesterone can relieve water retention while some synthetic progesto*gens* can cause water retention; (3) progesterone is converted into other hormones by the adrenal glands, while synthetic proges*togen* is not; (4) progesterone can be administered to the fetus, but progest*ogens* cause masculinization of the female fetus.[26]

How long does the treatment last?

Typically, the younger a woman, the less time she will require progesterone therapy. The older she is and the more children she has had, the longer she will require treatment. A woman under 30 who has not had a full-term pregnancy may require progesterone therapy for only 6 to 12 months. A woman over 40 who has had one or more pregnancies may require progesterone therapy until menopause.[27]

Is it possible to overdose with progesterone?

When a woman is pregnant, the progesterone level in her body rises 20 to 30 times higher than in a non-pregnant state. Moreover, the high progesterone level of pregnancy is maintained for a duration of 9 months, as compared to a raised (but much lower level) during her premenstrual phase. As Dr. Dalton points out, it is impossible for a woman who has been pregnant to overdose with progesterone. Most women who have not been pregnant are capable of dealing with the high levels that occur in pregnancy, thus the smaller dosage administered during progesterone therapy is not a problem. She notes that in a young girl who has never been pregnant, the effects of overdose are euphoria, restless energy, faintness and uterine cramps.[28]

What are the side effects?

The side effects of progesterone are uncommon and not very serious. They include:

- Shortening the cycle. This can be corrected by starting progesterone 1 or 2 days later during the next cycle.
- Lengthening the cycle. This is corrected by stopping progesterone at the time of expected menstruation, and bleeding will occur within 48 hours.
- Spotting at midcycle. This is corrected by not using progesterone too early in the cycle.
- Spotting in the premenstrual time. The correction for this is to stop progesterone, and start the next course of treatment 1 or 2 days later.
- Erratic cycles. This is corrected by administering progesterone systematically, as erratic cycles are an indication that the woman has forgotten to use progesterone for 1 or 2 days.
- Generalized skin rash. This is corrected by discontinuing injections and substituting suppositories. The rash is a reaction to the vegetable oil used in injectable progesterone.[29]

Can progesterone be taken with other medications?

Medical researchers tend to agree that progesterone has no absolute contraindications (times when one medication should not be used in combination with other medications).[30]

What do doctors say about progesterone therapy?

Despite the controversy around progesterone therapy, many doctors prescribe its use to treat the severe symptoms of PMS. Here is what medical doctors who are authorities on PMS say:

Dr. Susan Lark:

> *I have been using progesterone for the last few years in my medical practice, and have found it to have fewer side effects than the more commonly used drugs. . . I have seen excellent results in most of my patients who use it and strongly advocate its use in appropriate cases.*[31]

Dr. Niels Lauersen:

> *Progesterone is . . . indicated for women who are suffering from PMS symptoms severe enough to interfere with their daily routines. When marital and family lives are affected and the safety of children is at stake, progesterone should be administered. Progesterone is also suggested if there are signs that PMS may lead to suicide attempts, self-injury, increased alcohol consumption, or cyclic illness that requires hospitalization. Tortuous recurring migraines that cannot be curbed with other medications may provide another reason for progesterone therapy.*[32]

Dr. Michelle Harrison:

> *Progesterone, when it is effective, seems to prevent or alleviate the premenstrual symptoms so that the woman often feels 'like herself.' The drug does not produce the drowsiness or fogginess characteristic of tranquilizers. The woman who benefits from progesterone is not particularly aware of being on a drug. When the drug wears off, however, she suddenly becomes aware of the premenstrual symptoms.*[33]

Dr. Katharina Dalton:

> *It is important to appreciate that not all patients with premenstrual syndrome require progesterone therapy, nor is there any justification for treating with hormones those whose symptoms do not warrant treatment. There are, however, many women whose symptoms can be relieved only with progesterone and these women certainly need treating for their lives can be transformed.*[34] *When women with the premenstrual syndrome who have been treated with progesterone return to the doctor, it is often difficult to recognize them as the same women who first came for advice and treatment.*[35]

Dr. Suzanne Trupin:

> *[Progesterone therapy] has proved to be the chemical treatment of choice among physicians. Its simplicity lends itself to easy administration and monitoring. Almost uniformly patients report positive effects.*[36]

Dr. Ronald Norris:

> *At present, progesterone is recommended because it seems to be the most helpful agent for the multiple symptoms of PMS and because it appears to have the fewest significant side effects of any of the medications used for PMS.*[37]

Adding to these testimonials by medical doctors, I find that women who have previously worked unsuccessfully with prescription medications such as diuretics and tranquilizers have significant relief from their symptoms by using progesterone. I recognize that progesterone therapy is still somewhat controversial, but almost every one of my clients who has chosen treatment with progesterone has reported significant improvement in her PMS symptoms.

The first choice for treatment of PMS is always self-help—diet, vitamins and exercise. When these fail to achieve the desired results, progesterone is a reasonable alternative to consider.

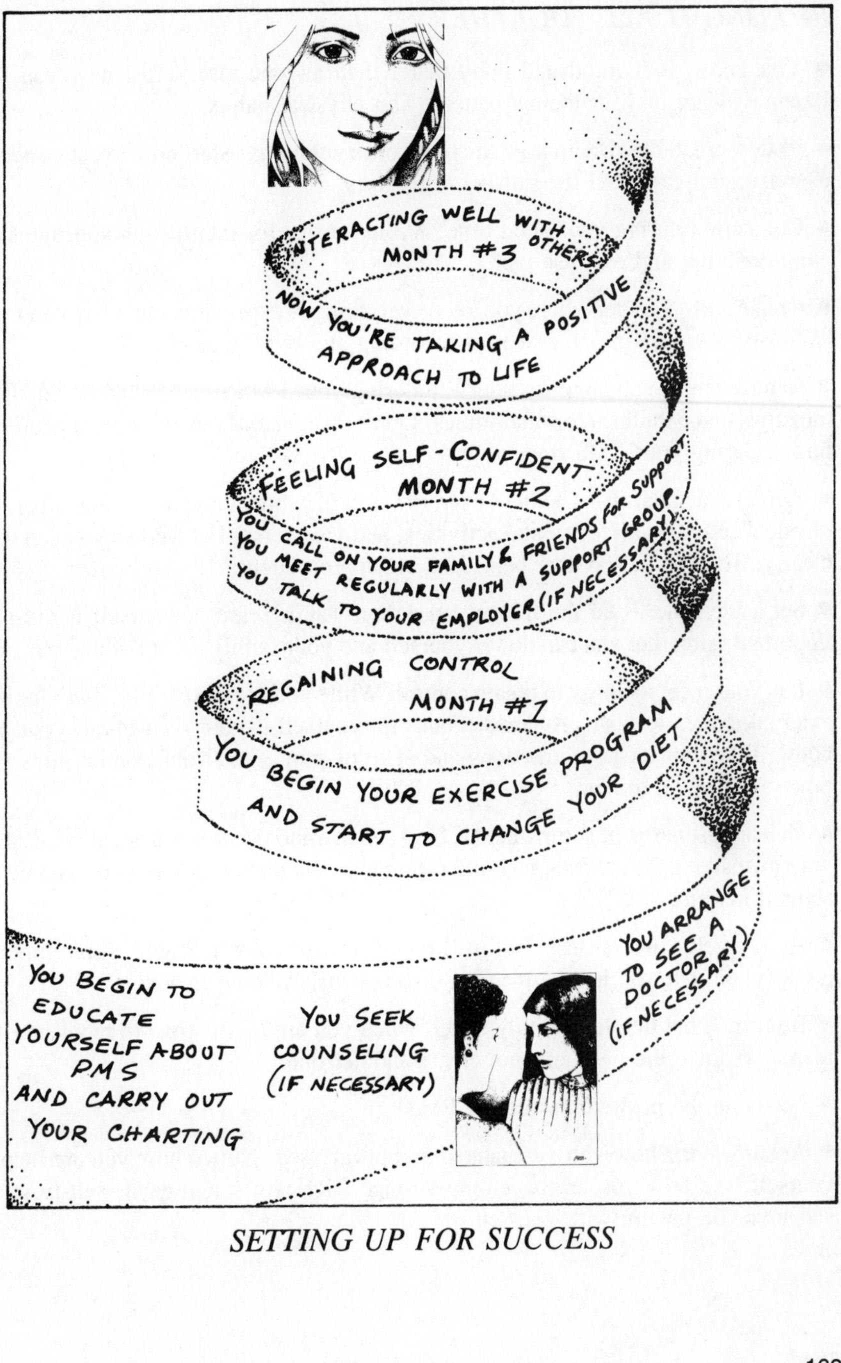
INTERACTING WELL WITH OTHERS
MONTH #3
NOW YOU'RE TAKING A POSITIVE APPROACH TO LIFE
FEELING SELF-CONFIDENT
MONTH #2
YOU CALL ON YOUR FAMILY & FRIENDS FOR SUPPORT
YOU MEET REGULARLY WITH A SUPPORT GROUP.
YOU TALK TO YOUR EMPLOYER (IF NECESSARY)
REGAINING CONTROL
MONTH #1
YOU BEGIN YOUR EXERCISE PROGRAM AND START TO CHANGE YOUR DIET
YOU ARRANGE TO SEE A DOCTOR (IF NECESSARY)
YOU BEGIN TO EDUCATE YOURSELF ABOUT PMS AND CARRY OUT YOUR CHARTING
YOU SEEK COUNSELING (IF NECESSARY)

SETTING UP FOR SUCCESS

PUTTING IT ALL TOGETHER

- You know your mind and body better than anyone else. Trust how you feel. Become aware of your mental patterns and physical habits.

- PMS is treatable. Begin now to chart your symptoms. Start now to eat correctly, exercise, and carry out the self-help exercises.

- Get started during your good time. Avoid set-ups for failure—in your thinking, emotions, diet and exercise plan.

- Create a PMS folder where you keep everything—especially your charts and your exercise records—in one place for recording and reinforcement.

- Reduce stress and simplify your life during your PMS time. Schedule important meetings and deadlines for other times. Don't take on extra work or extra people (at home) during your PMS time.

- Achieve a balance—in diet, exercise, sleep, work and play. Remember that physical activities affect mental activities, and vice versa. Eat well so you can think clearly. Think in a way that helps you eat appropriately.

- Set aside time to do the things you enjoy. Taking care of yourself is the most important thing that you can do for yourself and your family during your PMS time.

- It is your responsibility to regain control. While you are recovering, don't look for external causes to your problems. Focus on yourself—your own mind, your own body. Take care of your emotions and state of mind, and your relationships with others will begin to heal.

- You are in charge of getting better, but keep in mind that you are not alone. Call on your husband or lover, friends, family, therapist and doctor to help you. You need a support system.

- Assure your own professional well-being. If necessary, talk with your employer and explain that you have a medical disorder that is being treated.

- Be firm—but gentle—with yourself when you are on the road to recovery. The idea is to solve the problem, not create another one.

- Focus on the positive in treating PMS!

- Acknowledge how you've changed and progressed. Notice how you are helping yourself, see how you are becoming stronger. Relearn self-respect, self-trust and self-love. Be patient with yourself.

Footnotes

[1]Katharina Dalton, *The Premenstrual Syndrome and Progesterone Therapy*, Second Edition, Year Book Medical Publishers, Inc., Chicago, 1984, p. viii.

[2]David R. Rubinow and Peter Roy-Byrne, "Premenstrual Syndromes: Overview From a Methodologic Perspective," *American Journal of Psychiatry*, Vol. 141, No. 2, February 1984, p. 163.

[3]John F. Steege, M.D., Anna L.Stout, Ph.D., and Sharon L. Rupp, R.N.C., "Relationships Among Premenstrual Symptoms and Menstrual Cycle Characteristics," *Obstetrics & Gynecology*, Vol. 65, No. 3, March 1985, pp. 398-402.

[4]Katharina Dalton, M.D., *The Premenstrual Syndrome and Progesterone Therapy*, Second Edition, Year Book Medical Publishers, Inc., Chicago, 1984, p. 52.

[5]*Journal of the American Medical Association*, Vol. 245, No. 14, April 10, 1981, p. 1393.

[6]D.R. Rubinow, M.D., quoted in "New PMS Theories," *The Washington Post*, February 19, 1986, p. 17.

[7]Katharina Dalton, M.D., *Once A Month*, Hunter House, Inc. Publishers, Claremont, California, 1983, p. 72.

[8]D.R. Rubinow, M.D. and Peter Roy-Byrne, M.D., "Premenstrual Syndromes: Overview From A Methodological Perspective," *American Journal of Psychiatry*, Vol. 141, No. 2, 1984, p. 168.

[9]Robert L. Reid, M.D. and S.S.C. Yen, M.D., *American Journal of Obstetrics and Gynecology*, Vol. 139, No. 85, 1981, p. 97.

[10]"Premenstrual Syndrome: An Ancient Woe Deserving of Modern Scrutiny," *Journal of the American Medical Association*, Vol. 245, April 10, 1981, p. 1393.

[11]I.K. Kroanyi, "Somatic Illness in Psychiatric Patients," *Psychosomatics*, Vol. 21, No. 11, 1980, pp. 887-891.

[12]This analysis is drawn from Daphne Chellos, "Premenstrual Syndrome: Considerations for Mental Health Professionals," unpublished manuscript, Department

of Education, University of Colorado, 1984, 19 pp. See also: R.C.W. Hall, E. Gardner, M.K. Popkin, A.F. LeCann, E. Stickney, "Unrecognized Physical Illness Prompting Psychiatric Admissions: A Prospective Study," *American Journal of Psychiatry,* Vol. 5, No. 138, 1981, pp. 629-635.

[13]Katharina Dalton, *The Premenstrual Syndrome and Progesterone Therapy,* Second Edition, Year Book Medical Publishers, Inc., Chicago, 1984, p. 24.

[14]James Scala, *Alive!,* Shaklee Corporation, October 1985.

[15]David R. Rubinow, M.D., Peter Roy-Byrne, M.D., *et al.,* "Prospective Assessment of Menstrually Related Mood Disorders," *American Journal of Psychiatry,* Vol. 141, No. 5, May 1984, p. 685.

[16]Ronald V. Norris, M.D., "Progesterone for Premenstrual Tension," *The Journal of Reproductive Medicine*, Vol. 28, No. 8, August 1983, p. 511.

[17]Robert L. Reid and S.S.C. Yen, "Premenstrual Syndrome," *American Journal of Obstetrics and Gynecology*, Vol. 139, No. 85, 1981, p. 97.

[18]Ronald V. Norris, M.D., "Progesterone for Premenstrual Tension," *The Journal of Reproductive Medicine*, Vol. 28, No. 8, August 1983, p. 509.

[19]R.L. Reid and S.C.C. Yen, "Premenstrual Syndrome," *American Journal of Obstetrics and Gynecology*, Vol. 139, No. 85, 1981, pp. 85-104. See also: 0. Janiger, R. Riffenburgh, and R. Kersh, "Cross Cultural Study of Premenstrual Syndromes," *Psychosomatics,* 13, July-August, 1972, pp. 226-234.

[20]Renate DeJong, Ph.D., David R. Rubinow, M.D., Peter Roy-Byrne, M.D., M. Christine Hoban, M.S.W., Gay N. Grover, M.S.N., and Robert M. Post, M.D., "Premenstrual Mood Disorder and Psychiatric Illness," *American Journal of Psychiatry*, Vol. 142, No. 11, November 1985, pp. 1359-1361.

[21]Watkins, Linda, "Premenstrual Distress Gains Notice As a Chronic Issue in the Workplace," *The Wall Street Journal,* January 22, 1986, p. 31.

[22]Katharina Dalton, M.D., *The Premenstrual Syndrome and Progesterone Therapy*, Second Edition, Year Book Medical Publishers, Inc., Chicago, 1984, pp. 74-75.

[23]Katharina Dalton, M.D., *The Premenstrual Syndrome and Progesterone Therapy*, Second Edition, Year Book Medical Publishers, Inc., Chicago, 1984, p. 133.

[24]Ronald V. Norris, M.D., "Progesterone for Premenstrual Tension," *The Journal of Reproductive Medicine*, Vol. 28, No. 8, August 1983, p. 514.

[25]Katharina Dalton, M.D., *A Guide to Progesterone Therapy for Premenstrual Syndrome,* PMS Action, Irvine, California, 1981, p. 5.

[26]Katharina Dalton, M.D., *A Guide to Progesterone Therapy for Premenstrual Syndrome*, PMS Action, Irvine, California, 1981, p. 6.

[27]Katharina Dalton, M.D., *A Guide to Progesterone Therapy for Premenstrual Syndrome,* PMS Action, Irvine, California, 1981, p. 4.

[28]Katharina Dalton, *A Guide to Progesterone Therapy for Premenstrual Syndrome*, PMS Action, Irvine, California, 1981, p. 5.

[29]Ronald V. Norris, M.D., "Progesterone for Premenstrual Tension," *Journal of Reproductive Medicine,* Vol. 28, No. 8, August 1983, p. 514.

[30]Katharina Dalton, M.D., *The Premenstrual Syndrome and Progesterone Therapy*, Second Edition, Year Book Medical Publishers, Inc., Chicago, 1984, p. 139.

[31]Susan Lark, M.D., *Premenstrual Syndrome Self-Help Book*, Formen Publishing, Inc., Los Angeles, California, 1984, p. 221.

[32]Niels H. Lauersen, M.D., and Eileen Stukane, *Premenstrual Syndrome and You*, Simon & Schuster, Inc., New York, 1983, p. 167.

[33]Michelle Harrison, M.D., *Self-Help for Premenstrual Syndrome*, Matrix Press, Cambridge, Massachusettes, 1984, p. 36.

[34]Katharina Dalton, M.D., *The Premenstrual Syndrome and Progesterone Therapy*, Second Edition, Year Book Medical Publishers, Inc., Chicago, 1984, p. 141.

[35]Katharina Dalton, M.D., *Once* a *Month*, Hunter House, Claremont, California, p. 179.

[36]Suzanne Trupin, M.D., *PMS: A Personal Workbook*, Second Edition, Champaign, Illinois, 1985, p. 121.

[37]Ronald V. Norris, M.D., "Progesterone for Premenstrual Tension," *The Journal of Reproductive Medicine*, Vol. 28, No. 8, August 1983, pp. 511-512.

Resources for Information About PMS

MEDICAL ARTICLES ABOUT PMS

Causes of PMS

Katharina Dalton, M.D., *The Premenstrual Syndrome and Progesterone Therapy*, Second Edition, Year Book Medical Publishers, Inc., Chicago, Illinois, 1984.

R.L. Reid, M.D. and S.C.C. Yen, M.D., "Premenstrual Syndrome," *American Journal of Obstetrics and Gynecology*, Vol. 139, No. 1, 1981, pp. 85-104.

David R. Rubinow, M.D., and Peter Roy-Byrne, M.D., "Premenstrual Syndromes: Overview from a Methodologic Perspective," *American Journal of Psychiatry*, Vol. 141, No. 2, February 1984, pp. 163-172.

PMS and Menstrual Cramps

John F. Steege, M.D., Anna L. Stout, Ph.D., and Sharon L. Rupp, R.N.C., "Relationships Among Premenstrual Symptoms and Menstrual Cycle Characteristics," *Obstetrics & Gynecology*, Vol. 65, No. 3, March 1985, pp. 398-402.

Penny W. Budoff, M.D., *No More Menstrual Cramps and Other Good News*, Penguin, New York, 1980.

PMS and Psychiatric Illness

Renate DeJong, Ph.D., David R. Rubinow, M.D., Peter Roy-Byrne, M.D., M. Christine Hoban, M.S.W., Gay N. Grover, M.S.N., and Robert M. Post, M.D., "Premenstrual Mood Disorder and Psychiatric Illness," *American Journal of Psychiatry*, Vol. 142, No. 11, November 1985, pp. 1359-1361.

David R. Rubinow, M.D., Christine Hoban, M.S.W., Peter Roy-Byrne, M.D., Gay N. Grover, M.S.N., and Robert M. Post, M.D., "Premenstrual Syndromes: Past and Future Research Strategies," *Canadian Journal of Psychiatry*, Vol. 30, November 1985, pp. 469-473.

PMS and Psychological Assessment

Anna L. Stout, Ph.D., and John F. Steege, M.D., "Psychological Assessment of Women Seeking Treatment for Premenstrual Syndrome," *Journal of Psychosomatic Research,* Vol. 29, No. 6, 1985, pp. 621-629.

PMS and Progesterone

Katharina Dalton, M.D., *The Premenstrual Syndrome and Progesterone Therapy*, Second Edition, Year Book Medical Publishers, Inc., Chicago, Illinois, 1984.

Ronald V. Norris, M.D., "Progesterone for Premenstrual Tension," *Journal of Reproductive Medicine*, Vol. 28, No. 8, August 1983, pp. 509-516.

PHARMACOLOGICAL ADVICE

Madison Pharmacy Associates
429 Gammon Place
Madison, Wisconsin 53719
1-800-558-7046

INFORMATION, COUNSELING, AND PRESENTATIONS

PreMenstrual Syndrome Clinic
2760 29th Street, Suite 205
Boulder, Colorado 80301
303-440-7100

PMS NEWSLETTER

PMS Access
P.O. Box 9326
Madison, Wisconsin 53715
1-800-222-4PMS

Your Daily Charts

Symptom #1 ______________________ Symptom #3 ______________________

Symptom #2 ______________________ Symptom #4 ______________________

Ratings: 0 (no symptoms), 1, 2, 3, 4, 5, 6, 7, 8, 9, 10 (most severe)

Month #1

1 _____ (date)

Symptom #1 ___ Comments: ______________________

Symptom #2 ___ ______________________

Symptom #3 ___ ______________________

Symptom #4 ___ ______________________

Food and beverage intake: ______________________

____

____

____

Exercise: ______________________

____

____

Comment on the day: ______________________

____

____

Overall rating for the day: ______________________

2 _____ (date)

Symptom #1 ___ Comments: ______________________

Symptom #2 ___ ______________________

Symptom #3 ___ ______________________

Symptom #4 ___ ______________________

Food and beverage intake: ______________________________

____

____

____

Exercise: ______________________________

____

____

Comment on the day: ______________________________

____

____

Overall rating for the day: ______________________________

3 _____ (date)

Symptom #1 ___ Comments: ______________________________

Symptom #2 ___ ______________________________

Symptom #3 ___ ______________________________

Symptom #4 ___ ______________________________

Food and beverage intake: ______________________________

____

____

____

Exercise: ______________________________

____

____

Comment on the day: ______________________________

____

____

Overall rating for the day: ______________________________

4 ______ Symptom #1 ___ Comments: ______________________________
(date)
Symptom #2 ___ ______________________________
Symptom #3 ___ ______________________________
Symptom #4 ___ ______________________________
Food and beverage intake: ______________________________
____
____
____
____
Exercise: ______________________________
____
____
Comment on the day: ______________________________
____
____
____
Overall rating for the day: ______________________________

5 ______ Symptom #1 ___ Comments: ______________________________
(date)
Symptom #2 ___ ______________________________
Symptom #3 ___ ______________________________
Symptom #4 ___ ______________________________
Food and beverage intake: ______________________________
____
____
____
____

Exercise: __________

Comment on the day: __________

Overall rating for the day: __________

6 _____ (date)

Symptom #1 __ Comments: __________

Symptom #2 __

Symptom #3 __

Symptom #4 __

Food and beverage intake: __________

Exercise: __________

Comment on the day: __________

Overall rating for the day: __________

7 ______ (date)

Symptom #1 ___ Comments: ______________________

Symptom #2 ___ ______________________

Symptom #3 ___ ______________________

Symptom #4 ___ ______________________

Food and beverage intake: ______________________

Exercise: ______________________

Comment on the day: ______________________

Overall rating for the day: ______________________

8 ______ (date)

Symptom #1 ___ Comments: ______________________

Symptom #2 ___ ______________________

Symptom #3 ___ ______________________

Symptom #4 ___ ______________________

Food and beverage intake: ______________________

Exercise: ______________________________

____

____

Comment on the day: ______________________________

____

____

____

Overall rating for the day: ______________________________

9 _____ Symptom #1 ___ Comments: ______________________________
(date)
Symptom #2 ___ ______________________________

Symptom #3 ___ ______________________________

Symptom #4 ___ ______________________________

Food and beverage intake: ______________________________

____

____

____

____

Exercise: ______________________________

____

____

Comment on the day: ______________________________

____

____

____

Overall rating for the day: ______________________________

10 ____ (date)

Symptom #1 ___ Comments: ____________________

Symptom #2 ___ ____________________

Symptom #3 ___ ____________________

Symptom #4 ___ ____________________

Food and beverage intake: ____________________

____

____

____

____

Exercise: ____________________

____

____

Comment on the day: ____________________

____

____

____

Overall rating for the day: ____________________

11 ____ (date)

Symptom #1 ___ Comments: ____________________

Symptom #2 ___ ____________________

Symptom #3 ___ ____________________

Symptom #4 ___ ____________________

Food and beverage intake: ____________________

____

____

____

____

Exercise: ______________________________

____

____

Comment on the day: ______________________________

____

____

____

Overall rating for the day: ______________________________

12 ____ Symptom #1 __ Comments: ______________________________
(date)
Symptom #2 __ ______________________________

Symptom #3 __ ______________________________

Symptom #4 __ ______________________________

Food and beverage intake: ______________________________

____

____

____

____

Exercise: ______________________________

____

____

Comment on the day: ______________________________

____

____

____

Overall rating for the day: ______________________________

13 ____ (date)

Symptom #1 ___ Comments: ____________________

Symptom #2 ___ ____________________

Symptom #3 ___ ____________________

Symptom #4 ___ ____________________

Food and beverage intake: ____________________

Exercise: ____________________

Comment on the day: ____________________

Overall rating for the day: ____________________

14 ____ (date)

Symptom #1 ___ Comments: ____________________

Symptom #2 ___ ____________________

Symptom #3 ___ ____________________

Symptom #4 ___ ____________________

Food and beverage intake: ____________________

Exercise: ______________________________

____

____

Comment on the day: ______________________________

____

____

____

Overall rating for the day: ______________________________

15 ____ (date) Symptom #1 ___ Comments: ______________________________

Symptom #2 ___ ______________________________

Symptom #3 ___ ______________________________

Symptom #4 ___ ______________________________

Food and beverage intake: ______________________________

____

____

____

____

Exercise: ______________________________

____

____

Comment on the day: ______________________________

____

____

____

Overall rating for the day: ______________________________

16 ____ (date)
Symptom #1 ___ Comments: ____________________
Symptom #2 ___ ____________________
Symptom #3 ___ ____________________
Symptom #4 ___ ____________________

Food and beverage intake: ____________________

____

____

____

____

Exercise: ____________________

____

____

Comment on the day: ____________________

____

____

____

Overall rating for the day: ____________________

17 ____ (date)
Symptom #1 ___ Comments: ____________________
Symptom #2 ___ ____________________
Symptom #3 ___ ____________________
Symptom #4 ___ ____________________

Food and beverage intake: ____________________

____

____

____

____

Exercise: ______________________________

____

____

Comment on the day: ______________________________

____

____

____

Overall rating for the day: ______________________________

18 ____ (date)

Symptom #1 __ Comments: ______________________________

Symptom #2 __ ______________________________

Symptom #3 __ ______________________________

Symptom #4 __ ______________________________

Food and beverage intake: ______________________________

____

____

____

____

Exercise: ______________________________

____

____

Comment on the day: ______________________________

____

____

____

Overall rating for the day: ______________________________

19 ____ (date)

Symptom #1 ___ Comments: ____________________

Symptom #2 ___ ____________________

Symptom #3 ___ ____________________

Symptom #4 ___ ____________________

Food and beverage intake: ____________________

Exercise: ____________________

Comment on the day: ____________________

Overall rating for the day: ____________________

20 ____ (date)

Symptom #1 ___ Comments: ____________________

Symptom #2 ___ ____________________

Symptom #3 ___ ____________________

Symptom #4 ___ ____________________

Food and beverage intake: ____________________

Exercise: ______________________________

____

____

Comment on the day: ______________________________

____

____

____

Overall rating for the day: ______________________________

21 ____ (date) Symptom #1 ___ Comments: ______________________________

Symptom #2 ___ ______________________________

Symptom #3 ___ ______________________________

Symptom #4 ___ ______________________________

Food and beverage intake: ______________________________

____

____

____

____

Exercise: ______________________________

____

____

Comment on the day: ______________________________

____

____

____

Overall rating for the day: ______________________________

22 ____ (date)

Symptom #1 ___ Comments: ____________________

Symptom #2 ___ ____________________

Symptom #3 ___ ____________________

Symptom #4 ___ ____________________

Food and beverage intake: ____________________

____

____

____

____

Exercise: ____________________

____

____

Comment on the day: ____________________

____

____

____

Overall rating for the day: ____________________

23 ____ (date)

Symptom #1 ___ Comments: ____________________

Symptom #2 ___ ____________________

Symptom #3 ___ ____________________

Symptom #4 ___ ____________________

Food and beverage intake: ____________________

____

____

____

____

Exercise: ______________________________

____

____

Comment on the day: ______________________________

____

____

____

Overall rating for the day: ______________________________

24 ____ (date)

Symptom #1 __ Comments: ______________________________

Symptom #2 __ ______________________________

Symptom #3 __ ______________________________

Symptom #4 __ ______________________________

Food and beverage intake: ______________________________

____

____

____

____

Exercise: ______________________________

____

____

Comment on the day: ______________________________

____

____

____

Overall rating for the day: ______________________________

25 ____ (date)

Symptom #1 ___ Comments: ______________________

Symptom #2 ___ ______________________

Symptom #3 ___ ______________________

Symptom #4 ___ ______________________

Food and beverage intake: ______________________

____

____

____

____

Exercise: ______________________

____

____

Comment on the day: ______________________

____

____

____

Overall rating for the day: ______________________

26 ____ (date)

Symptom #1 ___ Comments: ______________________

Symptom #2 ___ ______________________

Symptom #3 ___ ______________________

Symptom #4 ___ ______________________

Food and beverage intake: ______________________

____

____

____

____

Exercise: ______________________________

____

____

Comment on the day: ______________________________

____

____

____

Overall rating for the day: ______________________________

27 ____ (date)

Symptom #1 ___ Comments: ______________________________

Symptom #2 ___ ______________________________

Symptom #3 ___ ______________________________

Symptom #4 ___ ______________________________

Food and beverage intake: ______________________________

____

____

____

____

Exercise: ______________________________

____

____

Comment on the day: ______________________________

____

____

____

Overall rating for the day: ______________________________

28 ____ (date)

Symptom #1 ___ Comments: ____________________

Symptom #2 ___ ____________________

Symptom #3 ___ ____________________

Symptom #4 ___ ____________________

Food and beverage intake: ____________________

Exercise: ____________________

Comment on the day: ____________________

Overall rating for the day: ____________________

29 ____ (date)

Symptom #1 ___ Comments: ____________________

Symptom #2 ___ ____________________

Symptom #3 ___ ____________________

Symptom #4 ___ ____________________

Food and beverage intake: ____________________

Exercise: ______________________________

____

____

Comment on the day: ______________________________

____

____

____

Overall rating for the day: ______________________________

30 ____ (date) Symptom #1 __ Comments: ______________________________

Symptom #2 __ ______________________________

Symptom #3 __ ______________________________

Symptom #4 __ ______________________________

Food and beverage intake: ______________________________

____

____

____

____

Exercise: ______________________________

____

____

Comment on the day: ______________________________

____

____

____

Overall rating for the day: ______________________________

31 ____ (date)

Symptom #1 ___ Comments: ____________________

Symptom #2 ___ ____________________

Symptom #3 ___ ____________________

Symptom #4 ___ ____________________

Food and beverage intake: ____________________

____

____

____

____

Exercise: ____________________

____

____

Comment on the day: ____________________

____

____

____

Overall rating for the day: ____________________

Month #2

1 ____ (date)

Symptom #1 ___ Comments: ____________________

Symptom #2 ___ ____________________

Symptom #3 ___ ____________________

Symptom #4 ___ ____________________

Food and beverage intake: ____________________

____

____

____

Exercise: ____

____

____

Comment on the day: ____________________________________

____

____

____

Overall rating for the day: _____________________________

2 ______ (date)

Symptom #1 ___ Comments: _______________________________

Symptom #2 ___ ____

Symptom #3 ___ ____

Symptom #4 ___ ____

Food and beverage intake: ______________________________

____

____

____

____

Exercise: ____

____

____

Comment on the day: ____________________________________

____

____

____

Overall rating for the day: _____________________________

3 ______ (date) Symptom #1 ___ Comments: ____________________

Symptom #2 ___ ____________________

Symptom #3 ___ ____________________

Symptom #4 ___ ____________________

Food and beverage intake: ____________________

____

____

____

____

Exercise: ____________________

____

____

Comment on the day: ____________________

____

____

____

Overall rating for the day: ____________________

4 ______ (date) Symptom #1 ___ Comments: ____________________

Symptom #2 ___ ____________________

Symptom #3 ___ ____________________

Symptom #4 ___ ____________________

Food and beverage intake: ____________________

____

____

____

____

Exercise: ____________________

____

____

Comment on the day: ____________________

____

____

____

Overall rating for the day: ____________________

5 _____ (date)

Symptom #1 ___ Comments: ____________________

Symptom #2 ___ ____________________

Symptom #3 ___ ____________________

Symptom #4 ___ ____________________

Food and beverage intake: ____________________

____

____

____

____

Exercise: ____________________

____

____

Comment on the day: ____________________

____

____

____

Overall rating for the day: ____________________

6 ______ (date)

Symptom #1 ___ Comments: ______________________________

Symptom #2 ___ ______________________________

Symptom #3 ___ ______________________________

Symptom #4 ___ ______________________________

Food and beverage intake: ______________________________

____

____

____

____

Exercise: ______________________________

____

____

Comment on the day: ______________________________

____

____

____

Overall rating for the day: ______________________________

7 ______ (date)

Symptom #1 ___ Comments: ______________________________

Symptom #2 ___ ______________________________

Symptom #3 ___ ______________________________

Symptom #4 ___ ______________________________

Food and beverage intake: ______________________________

____

____

____

____

Exercise: ______________________________

____

____

Comment on the day: ______________________________

____

____

____

Overall rating for the day: ______________________________

8 _____ (date)

Symptom #1 ___ Comments: ______________________________

Symptom #2 ___ ______________________________

Symptom #3 ___ ______________________________

Symptom #4 ___ ______________________________

Food and beverage intake: ______________________________

____

____

____

____

Exercise: ______________________________

____

____

Comment on the day: ______________________________

____

____

____

Overall rating for the day: ______________________________

9 ______ (date)

Symptom #1 ___ Comments: ______________________________

Symptom #2 ___ ______________________________

Symptom #3 ___ ______________________________

Symptom #4 ___ ______________________________

Food and beverage intake: ______________________________

____

____

____

____

Exercise: ______________________________

____

____

Comment on the day: ______________________________

____

____

____

Overall rating for the day: ______________________________

10 ______ (date)

Symptom #1 ___ Comments: ______________________________

Symptom #2 ___ ______________________________

Symptom #3 ___ ______________________________

Symptom #4 ___ ______________________________

Food and beverage intake: ______________________________

____

____

____

____

Exercise: ______________________________

____

____

Comment on the day: ______________________________

____

____

____

Overall rating for the day: ______________________________

11 ____ (date) Symptom #1 __ Comments: ______________________________

Symptom #2 __ ______________________________

Symptom #3 __ ______________________________

Symptom #4 __ ______________________________

Food and beverage intake: ______________________________

____

____

____

____

Exercise: ______________________________

____

____

Comment on the day: ______________________________

____

____

____

Overall rating for the day: ______________________________

12 ____ (date)

Symptom #1 ___ Comments: ________________

Symptom #2 ___ ________________

Symptom #3 ___ ________________

Symptom #4 ___ ________________

Food and beverage intake: ________________

____

____

____

____

Exercise: ________________

____

____

Comment on the day: ________________

____

____

____

Overall rating for the day: ________________

13 ____ (date)

Symptom #1 ___ Comments: ________________

Symptom #2 ___ ________________

Symptom #3 ___ ________________

Symptom #4 ___ ________________

Food and beverage intake: ________________

____

____

____

____

Exercise: ______________________________

____

____

Comment on the day: ______________________________

____

____

____

Overall rating for the day: ______________________________

14 ____ (date)

Symptom #1 ___ Comments: ______________________________

Symptom #2 ___ ______________________________

Symptom #3 ___ ______________________________

Symptom #4 ___ ______________________________

Food and beverage intake: ______________________________

____

____

____

____

Exercise: ______________________________

____

____

Comment on the day: ______________________________

____

____

____

Overall rating for the day: ______________________________

15 ____ (date)
Symptom #1 ___ Comments: ____________________
Symptom #2 ___ ____________________
Symptom #3 ___ ____________________
Symptom #4 ___ ____________________
Food and beverage intake: ____________________

Exercise: ____________________

Comment on the day: ____________________

Overall rating for the day: ____________________

16 ____ (date)
Symptom #1 ___ Comments: ____________________
Symptom #2 ___ ____________________
Symptom #3 ___ ____________________
Symptom #4 ___ ____________________
Food and beverage intake: ____________________

Exercise: ______________________________

____

____

Comment on the day: ______________________________

____

____

____

Overall rating for the day: ______________________________

17 ____ Symptom #1 ___ Comments: ______________________________
(date)
Symptom #2 ___ ______________________________

Symptom #3 ___ ______________________________

Symptom #4 ___ ______________________________

Food and beverage intake: ______________________________

____

____

____

____

Exercise: ______________________________

____

____

Comment on the day: ______________________________

____

____

____

Overall rating for the day: ______________________________

18 ____ (date)

Symptom #1 ___ Comments: ______________________

Symptom #2 ___ ______________________

Symptom #3 ___ ______________________

Symptom #4 ___ ______________________

Food and beverage intake: ______________________

____

____

____

____

Exercise: ______________________

____

____

Comment on the day: ______________________

____

____

____

Overall rating for the day: ______________________

19 ____ (date)

Symptom #1 ___ Comments: ______________________

Symptom #2 ___ ______________________

Symptom #3 ___ ______________________

Symptom #4 ___ ______________________

Food and beverage intake: ______________________

____

____

____

____

Exercise: ______________________________

____

____

Comment on the day: ______________________________

____

____

____

Overall rating for the day: ______________________________

20 ____ (date)

Symptom #1 __ Comments: ______________________________

Symptom #2 __ ______________________________

Symptom #3 __ ______________________________

Symptom #4 __ ______________________________

Food and beverage intake: ______________________________

____

____

____

____

Exercise: ______________________________

____

____

Comment on the day: ______________________________

____

____

____

Overall rating for the day: ______________________________

21 ____ (date)

Symptom #1 __ Comments: __________

Symptom #2 __ __________

Symptom #3 __ __________

Symptom #4 __ __________

Food and beverage intake: __________

Exercise: __________

Comment on the day: __________

Overall rating for the day: __________

22 ____ (date)

Symptom #1 __ Comments: __________

Symptom #2 __ __________

Symptom #3 __ __________

Symptom #4 __ __________

Food and beverage intake: __________

Exercise: ______________________________

____

____

Comment on the day: ______________________________

____

____

____

Overall rating for the day: ______________________________

23 ____ (date)

Symptom #1 __ Comments: ______________________________

Symptom #2 __ ______________________________

Symptom #3 __ ______________________________

Symptom #4 __ ______________________________

Food and beverage intake: ______________________________

____

____

____

____

Exercise: ______________________________

____

____

Comment on the day: ______________________________

____

____

____

Overall rating for the day: ______________________________

24 ____ (date)

Symptom #1 ___ Comments: ____________________

Symptom #2 ___ ____________________

Symptom #3 ___ ____________________

Symptom #4 ___ ____________________

Food and beverage intake: ____________________

Exercise: ____________________

Comment on the day: ____________________

Overall rating for the day: ____________________

25 ____ (date)

Symptom #1 ___ Comments: ____________________

Symptom #2 ___ ____________________

Symptom #3 ___ ____________________

Symptom #4 ___ ____________________

Food and beverage intake: ____________________

Exercise: ____

____

____

Comment on the day: ________________________________

____

____

____

Overall rating for the day: ___________________________

26 ____ (date)

Symptom #1 ___ Comments: ______________________

Symptom #2 ___ ______________________

Symptom #3 ___ ______________________

Symptom #4 ___ ______________________

Food and beverage intake: ____________________________

____

____

____

____

Exercise: ____

____

____

Comment on the day: ________________________________

____

____

____

Overall rating for the day: ___________________________

27 ____ (date)

Symptom #1 ___ Comments: ________________

Symptom #2 ___ ________________

Symptom #3 ___ ________________

Symptom #4 ___ ________________

Food and beverage intake: ________________

Exercise: ________________

Comment on the day: ________________

Overall rating for the day: ________________

28 ____ (date)

Symptom #1 ___ Comments: ________________

Symptom #2 ___ ________________

Symptom #3 ___ ________________

Symptom #4 ___ ________________

Food and beverage intake: ________________

Exercise: ________________________________

____

____

Comment on the day: ________________________________

____

____

____

Overall rating for the day: ________________________________

29 ____ (date)

Symptom #1 ___ Comments: ________________________________

Symptom #2 ___ ________________________________

Symptom #3 ___ ________________________________

Symptom #4 ___ ________________________________

Food and beverage intake: ________________________________

____

____

____

____

Exercise: ________________________________

____

____

Comment on the day: ________________________________

____

____

____

Overall rating for the day: ________________________________

30 ____ (date)

Symptom #1 ___ Comments: ____________________

Symptom #2 ___ ____________________

Symptom #3 ___ ____________________

Symptom #4 ___ ____________________

Food and beverage intake: ____________________

____

____

____

____

Exercise: ____________________

____

____

Comment on the day: ____________________

____

____

____

Overall rating for the day: ____________________

31 ____ (date)

Symptom #1 ___ Comments: ____________________

Symptom #2 ___ ____________________

Symptom #3 ___ ____________________

Symptom #4 ___ ____________________

Food and beverage intake: ____________________

____

____

____

____

Exercise: ______________________________

____

____

Comment on the day: ______________________________

____

____

____

Overall rating for the day: ______________________________

Month #3

1 _____ (date)

Symptom #1 ___ Comments: ______________________________

Symptom #2 ___ ______________________________

Symptom #3 ___ ______________________________

Symptom #4 ___ ______________________________

Food and beverage intake: ______________________________

____

____

____

____

Exercise: ______________________________

____

____

Comment on the day: ______________________________

____

____

____

Overall rating for the day: ______________________________

2 ______ Symptom #1 ___ Comments: ______________________
(date)
Symptom #2 ___ ______________________
Symptom #3 ___ ______________________
Symptom #4 ___ ______________________

Food and beverage intake: ______________________

Exercise: ______________________

Comment on the day: ______________________

Overall rating for the day: ______________________

3 ______ Symptom #1 ___ Comments: ______________________
(date)
Symptom #2 ___ ______________________
Symptom #3 ___ ______________________
Symptom #4 ___ ______________________

Food and beverage intake: ______________________

Exercise: ______________________________

____

____

Comment on the day: ______________________________

____

____

____

Overall rating for the day: ______________________________

4 ______ (date)

Symptom #1 __ Comments: ______________________________

Symptom #2 __ ______________________________

Symptom #3 __ ______________________________

Symptom #4 __ ______________________________

Food and beverage intake: ______________________________

____

____

____

____

Exercise: ______________________________

____

____

Comment on the day: ______________________________

____

____

____

Overall rating for the day: ______________________________

5 _____ (date)

Symptom #1 ___ Comments: ______________________

Symptom #2 ___ ______________________

Symptom #3 ___ ______________________

Symptom #4 ___ ______________________

Food and beverage intake: ______________________

____

____

____

____

Exercise: ______________________

____

____

Comment on the day: ______________________

____

____

____

Overall rating for the day: ______________________

6 _____ (date)

Symptom #1 ___ Comments: ______________________

Symptom #2 ___ ______________________

Symptom #3 ___ ______________________

Symptom #4 ___ ______________________

Food and beverage intake: ______________________

____

____

____

____

Exercise: ______________________________

____

____

Comment on the day: ______________________________

____

____

____

Overall rating for the day: ______________________________

7 _____ (date)

Symptom #1 ___ Comments: ______________________________

Symptom #2 ___ ______________________________

Symptom #3 ___ ______________________________

Symptom #4 ___ ______________________________

Food and beverage intake: ______________________________

____

____

____

____

Exercise: ______________________________

____

____

Comment on the day: ______________________________

____

____

____

Overall rating for the day: ______________________________

8 ______ Symptom #1 ___ Comments: ______________________
(date) Symptom #2 ___ ______________________
Symptom #3 ___ ______________________
Symptom #4 ___ ______________________
Food and beverage intake: ______________________
____
____
____
____
Exercise: ______________________
____
____
Comment on the day: ______________________
____
____
____
Overall rating for the day: ______________________

9 ______ Symptom #1 ___ Comments: ______________________
(date) Symptom #2 ___ ______________________
Symptom #3 ___ ______________________
Symptom #4 ___ ______________________
Food and beverage intake: ______________________
____
____
____
____

Exercise: ______________________________

____

____

Comment on the day: ______________________________

____

____

____

Overall rating for the day: ______________________________

10 ____ (date)

Symptom #1 ___ Comments: ______________________________

Symptom #2 ___ ______________________________

Symptom #3 ___ ______________________________

Symptom #4 ___ ______________________________

Food and beverage intake: ______________________________

____

____

____

____

Exercise: ______________________________

____

____

Comment on the day: ______________________________

____

____

____

Overall rating for the day: ______________________________

11 ____ (date) Symptom #1 ___ Comments: ____________________

Symptom #2 ___ ____________________

Symptom #3 ___ ____________________

Symptom #4 ___ ____________________

Food and beverage intake: ____________________

Exercise: ____________________

Comment on the day: ____________________

Overall rating for the day: ____________________

12 ____ (date) Symptom #1 ___ Comments: ____________________

Symptom #2 ___ ____________________

Symptom #3 ___ ____________________

Symptom #4 ___ ____________________

Food and beverage intake: ____________________

Exercise: ______________________________

____

____

Comment on the day: ______________________________

____

____

____

Overall rating for the day: ______________________________

13 ____ (date)

Symptom #1 ___ Comments: ______________________________

Symptom #2 ___ ______________________________

Symptom #3 ___ ______________________________

Symptom #4 ___ ______________________________

Food and beverage intake: ______________________________

____

____

____

____

Exercise: ______________________________

____

____

Comment on the day: ______________________________

____

____

____

Overall rating for the day: ______________________________

14 ____ (date)

Symptom #1 ___ Comments: ________________

Symptom #2 ___ ________________

Symptom #3 ___ ________________

Symptom #4 ___ ________________

Food and beverage intake: ________________

Exercise: ________________

Comment on the day: ________________

Overall rating for the day: ________________

15 ____ (date)

Symptom #1 ___ Comments: ________________

Symptom #2 ___ ________________

Symptom #3 ___ ________________

Symptom #4 ___ ________________

Food and beverage intake: ________________

Exercise: ______________________________

____

____

Comment on the day: ______________________________

____

____

____

Overall rating for the day: ______________________________

16 ____ (date)

Symptom #1 ___ Comments: ______________________________

Symptom #2 ___ ______________________________

Symptom #3 ___ ______________________________

Symptom #4 ___ ______________________________

Food and beverage intake: ______________________________

____

____

____

____

Exercise: ______________________________

____

____

Comment on the day: ______________________________

____

____

____

Overall rating for the day: ______________________________

17 ____ (date) Symptom #1 ___ Comments: ____________________

Symptom #2 ___ ____________________

Symptom #3 ___ ____________________

Symptom #4 ___ ____________________

Food and beverage intake: ____________________

Exercise: ____________________

Comment on the day: ____________________

Overall rating for the day: ____________________

18 ____ (date) Symptom #1 ___ Comments: ____________________

Symptom #2 ___ ____________________

Symptom #3 ___ ____________________

Symptom #4 ___ ____________________

Food and beverage intake: ____________________

Exercise: ____________________

____

____

Comment on the day: ____________________

____

____

____

Overall rating for the day: ____________________

19 ____ (date)

Symptom #1 __ Comments: ____________________

Symptom #2 __ ____________________

Symptom #3 __ ____________________

Symptom #4 __ ____________________

Food and beverage intake: ____________________

____

____

____

____

Exercise: ____________________

____

____

Comment on the day: ____________________

____

____

____

Overall rating for the day: ____________________

20 ____ (date)
Symptom #1 ___ Comments: ____________________
Symptom #2 ___ ____________________
Symptom #3 ___ ____________________
Symptom #4 ___ ____________________

Food and beverage intake: ____________________

____

____

____

____

Exercise: ____________________

____

____

Comment on the day: ____________________

____

____

____

Overall rating for the day: ____________________

21 ____ (date)
Symptom #1 ___ Comments: ____________________
Symptom #2 ___ ____________________
Symptom #3 ___ ____________________
Symptom #4 ___ ____________________

Food and beverage intake: ____________________

____

____

____

____

Exercise: ______________________________

____

____

Comment on the day: ______________________________

____

____

____

Overall rating for the day: ______________________________

22 ____ (date)

Symptom #1 ___ Comments: ______________________________

Symptom #2 ___ ______________________________

Symptom #3 ___ ______________________________

Symptom #4 ___ ______________________________

Food and beverage intake: ______________________________

____

____

____

____

Exercise: ______________________________

____

____

Comment on the day: ______________________________

____

____

____

Overall rating for the day: ______________________________

23 ____ (date)

Symptom #1 ___ Comments: ____________________

Symptom #2 ___ ____________________

Symptom #3 ___ ____________________

Symptom #4 ___ ____________________

Food and beverage intake: ____________________

Exercise: ____________________

Comment on the day: ____________________

Overall rating for the day: ____________________

24 ____ (date)

Symptom #1 ___ Comments: ____________________

Symptom #2 ___ ____________________

Symptom #3 ___ ____________________

Symptom #4 ___ ____________________

Food and beverage intake: ____________________

Exercise: ______________________________

____

____

Comment on the day: ______________________________

____

____

____

Overall rating for the day: ______________________________

25 ____ (date)

Symptom #1 ___ Comments: ______________________________

Symptom #2 ___ ______________________________

Symptom #3 ___ ______________________________

Symptom #4 ___ ______________________________

Food and beverage intake: ______________________________

____

____

____

____

Exercise: ______________________________

____

____

Comment on the day: ______________________________

____

____

____

Overall rating for the day: ______________________________

26 ____ (date)

Symptom #1 ___ Comments: ____________________

Symptom #2 ___ ____________________

Symptom #3 ___ ____________________

Symptom #4 ___ ____________________

Food and beverage intake: ____________________

____

____

____

____

Exercise: ____________________

____

____

Comment on the day: ____________________

____

____

____

Overall rating for the day: ____________________

27 ____ (date)

Symptom #1 ___ Comments: ____________________

Symptom #2 ___ ____________________

Symptom #3 ___ ____________________

Symptom #4 ___ ____________________

Food and beverage intake: ____________________

____

____

____

____

Exercise: ______________________________

____

____

Comment on the day: ______________________________

____

____

____

Overall rating for the day: ______________________________

28 ____ (date)

Symptom #1 ___ Comments: ______________________________

Symptom #2 ___ ______________________________

Symptom #3 ___ ______________________________

Symptom #4 ___ ______________________________

Food and beverage intake: ______________________________

____

____

____

____

Exercise: ______________________________

____

____

Comment on the day: ______________________________

____

____

____

Overall rating for the day: ______________________________

29 ____ (date)

Symptom #1 ___ Comments: ________________________________

Symptom #2 ___ ________________________________

Symptom #3 ___ ________________________________

Symptom #4 ___ ________________________________

Food and beverage intake: ________________________________

____

____

____

____

Exercise: ________________________________

____

____

Comment on the day: ________________________________

____

____

____

Overall rating for the day: ________________________________

30 ____ (date)

Symptom #1 ___ Comments: ________________________________

Symptom #2 ___ ________________________________

Symptom #3 ___ ________________________________

Symptom #4 ___ ________________________________

Food and beverage intake: ________________________________

____

____

____

____

Exercise: ______________________________

____

____

Comment on the day: ______________________________

____

____

____

Overall rating for the day: ______________________________

31 ____ (date) Symptom #1 ___ Comments: ______________________________

Symptom #2 ___ ______________________________

Symptom #3 ___ ______________________________

Symptom #4 ___ ______________________________

Food and beverage intake: ______________________________

____

____

____

____

Exercise: ______________________________

____

____

Comment on the day: ______________________________

____

____

____

Overall rating for the day: ______________________________

Your On-Sight Chart

Day #	Month #1	Month #2	Month #3
1			
2			
3			
4			
5			
6			
7			
8			
9			
10			
11			
12			
13			
14			
15			
16			
17			
18			
19			
20			
21			
22			
23			
24			
25			
26			
27			
28			
29			
30			

Your Mood Chart

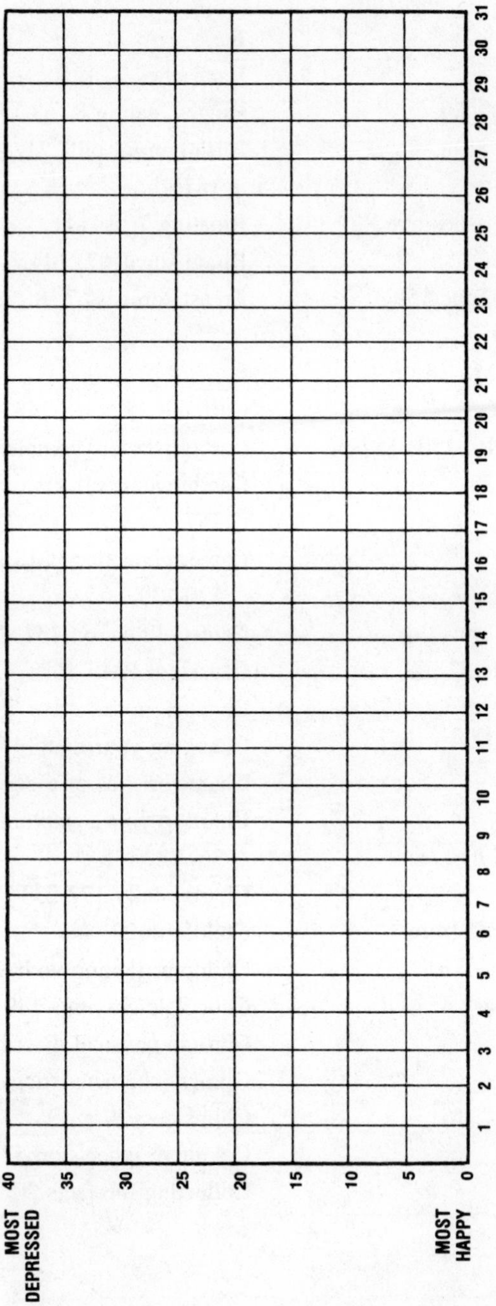

Index

About the Authors

Stephanie DeGraff Bender established the PMS Clinic in Boulder, Colorado in 1983. The clinic serves women who suspect they have PMS and are in need of assistance. Since 1983 the focus of the clinic has broadened to include family needs as well as individual needs. The clinic also sponsors workshops and seminars to educate the professional and lay communities.

Stephanie earned a B.A. degree in psychology from the University of Colorado at Boulder and a M.A. degree in clinical psychology from Antioch University. She has been active in women's health education issues, including teaching Lamaze childbirth preparation classes for four years.

Stephanie is married to Bill Bender, and they have two teen-aged sons, Billy and Tim.

Kathleen Kelleher is a freelance writer. She has written about many different topics, including the family, politics, and communications. Her publications include a book entitled *Teleconferencing: Linking People Together Electronically* (Prentice-Hall, Inc., 1985), academic monographs, magazine articles, and some fiction.

Kathleen lives in Boulder, Colorado with her son, Eric.